WORD HUNTERS

THE CURIOUS DICTIONARY

NICK EARLS &
TERRY WHIDBORNE

UQP

First published 2012 by University of Queensland Press
PO Box 6042, St Lucia, Queensland 4067 Australia
Reprinted 2013 (twice), 2014, 2016, 2021

www.uqp.com.au
uqp@uqp.uq.edu.au

Typeset in 11/16pt Horley Old Style by Jo Hunt
Printed in Australia by McPherson's Printing Group

Cataloguing-in-Publication Data
National Library of Australia

Earls, Nick, 1963-
The curious dictionary / by Nick Earls and Terry Whidborne.

Earls, Nick, 1963- Word hunters ; Book 1.

For primary school age.

Whidborne, Terry.

ISBN (pbk) 978 0 7022 4945 7
ISBN (pdf) 978 0 7022 4876 4
ISBN (epub) 978 0 7022 4878 8
ISBN (kindle) 978 0 7022 4879 5

A823.3

University of Queensland Press uses papers that are natural, renewable and
recyclable products made from wood grown in sustainable forests.
The logging and manufacturing processes conform to the environmental
regulations of the country of origin.

While stories build from words, it's true,

The words themselves have stories too.

Who dares to read? Who dares to look?

Who dares to hunt within this book?

*T*HE OLD MAN spoke in the past language one last time, to hear it again before it lapsed into silence. He thought of the kings he had served and lost, and the waste of it. He put the new words in his head instead, and set out to do his best with them, and for them.

With the knowledge he had gathered, he made the book.

It would not win the lost wars of his century, nor stop the myths and stories that would sweep in once its history was gone. It was a book for the future, bound by the last skilled act of old hands, to be sent into the world while it was still becoming. The book would remember, and learn, and seek. It was his best hope.

He set his needle down and checked the binding with his lens. He put away the scrolls and his instruments, and doused the fire.

And he walked into the woods late in his hundredth year and found a young hunter and gave him the book, saying, '*Ágoe þéos, begíme hit hwonne á beneþ þú. Íc i betimbrede hit ne æltæwee. Hit beþearfaþ þú and éow cynn á.*' 'Take this and heed it when it calls you, for I haven't made it well enough and it will need you and your kind, always.'

With that, his work was done.

Hello:
greeting (esp on telephone)

exclamation to draw attention

(variant of hallo, hullo).

& MORE

LEXI STILL HAD a buzzing in her head. She looked around, but she couldn't recognise anything. There was something wrong. She and Al were at the edge of a road, but it was more like a road from a movie or a museum. There was a carriage in the distance being pulled by horses and, standing almost as far away, a couple talking. The woman was wearing a bonnet and a full skirt that reached to the ground behind her. The man laughed at something she said, then slipped his hand inside his long coat and brought out a watch on a chain. Everything was drifting in and out of focus.

'What happened?' Al said. He was sitting next to Lexi, with his hands on the gravel to steady himself. 'How did that not kill us, whatever it was?'

'I don't know,' she said, 'but I'm pretty sure you started it.' She was his older sister by five minutes and, between the Hunter twins, it was always important to be clear about who started anything.

There was a noise from Al's bag – a ratty rustling and a clanking sound.

'It was Doug who started it,' Al said.

It was true, in a way, though it didn't seem fair to blame the whole thing on a pet rat. Doug had escaped from Al's bag and run into the part of the school library that was being

1

renovated, and that was marked off by barriers and a sign that said 'Out of Bounds'. Doug had raced ahead to a hole in the wall where a loose panel had moved, and it had been Al's hand that found the book when he had reached inside to grab him. The title on the cover read *Walker & Fuller's Curious Dictionary of English*.

The book had started to buzz, and a glow had come from somewhere inside it. It was Al who had called Lexi in to show her. It was Al who had opened the book to find the source of the glow. And Al who had pressed the golden button marked '& more' at the end of the definition of the word 'Hello'. At that point, things had stopped making sense.

'The library.' Lexi was trying to work it out. 'I don't know where the library is, but did we fall out of the sky to get here? And then just land, as if people can do that. As if you can fall thousands of metres and just land! You saw that too, didn't you – the world from high up?'

'Yes.' Al still felt dizzy.

A fog had rolled in, the library floor had dropped away and they had plunged through cloud and then open sky above this country that looked completely weird.

'So, this is, like, a village somewhere,' Lexi said, trying to put it all together. The nearest house was two storeys high and made of timber, with two chimneys rising from its peaked roof and a horse chewing grass near the front gate. Beyond it were two houses that were still being built, but work seemed to have finished for the day. 'We're nowhere near home. These are cold-climate houses. Look. They catch the sun, not the breeze. There's no shade. They've all got chimneys.' Their father was an architect, and always talking about breezes. 'Did you recognise anything on the way down? Oh, no, wait a second – that was when you had your hands over your face and you were screaming like a baby.'

'Because I was *plummeting to my death,*' Al said. 'Not because my Harry Potter poster got ripped.'

'That was—' She stopped herself. This was not the time to argue about her Harry Potter poster, or point out that it was authentic, from the first movie. She couldn't see her knees, she realised. Her lap was full of skirt. 'Hey, what am I wearing? How did there get to be a costume change?'

3

Lexi's long skirt went all the way down to lace-up boots and her sleeves ended in lace at the wrist. Her collar was lace too, and she was wearing a cameo brooch with a woman's face in white on a pale blue background. Lexi collected old brooches and made her own badges – she was regularly told to stop wearing them at school – but the cameo looked like something a grandma would wear. Her hair was different, too. She usually wore it in a ponytail, but now it was gathered and twisted into a kind of knot at the back of her head, with some hair falling to her neck in short ringlets.

'I'd never wear this,' she said, picking up the folds of the skirt and letting them drop again. 'Any of this. This is so embarrassing. And also totally weird.'

But Al wasn't going to be paying out on her for what she was wearing. He had a cap on, and a short jacket. Together they had the look of a uniform, but nothing like the school uniform he had been wearing seconds before. His boots were heavy and worn, with an old lace in one and string in the other. The really odd feature, though, was the pants, which puffed out until they were just below his knees and then tucked into socks, or maybe bandages. Whatever was holding the bottom of the pants in place seemed to be wound around his legs. He crossed them, hoping that they might look different. They didn't. Worse maybe. He uncrossed them.

'Even my bag's changed,' he said, as he took it from his shoulder. It was more of a satchel now, and closed by two buckles. 'There's something else in it, too.'

The bag made a clanking noise as Al put it down in his lap. He undid the first buckle and Doug jumped out, scrambled up to his shoulder and looked about, sniffing the air.

'Not sure I'd be brave enough to show my face around here if I were you,' Lexi said to him, but Doug was too busy counting smells – pine trees, a lavender-scented woman, birds, delicious horse poo and, somewhere, a warm pie made with fresh apples.

Al undid the second buckle and lifted the flap. His schoolbooks were still in there, but they were now wrapped in brown paper and tied up with string. There was something new as well.

Under the books were four golden pegs, the length of tent pegs but fatter. He lifted one out to take a look at it. It had levers on its sides, and it came to a point. At the other end, there was a small key fitted into a keyhole cut into ruby-coloured glass. Lexi reached in and took one too.

'What is this?' she said. 'Is it for some dorky wizard role-play game you and your friends are into? Or have these just appeared?'

'They've just appeared.'

'I'm ready for this to be a dream now,' she said. 'This is just stupid.'

She closed her eyes, but when she opened them nothing was different. Nothing other than the glowing writing on the new peg Al was holding.

'I saw it in the bag,' he said when he noticed her eyes

6

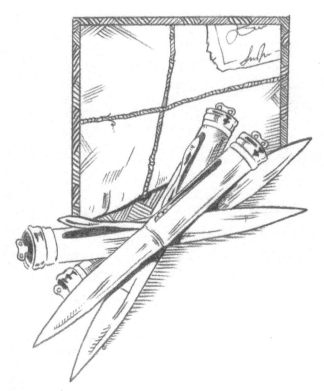

were open. He stared at the writing. 'I was just putting the other one back.'

'What does it say?'

He couldn't bring himself to read it aloud. He turned the peg so that Lexi could see it properly. The writing read, '1877, Menlo Park, New Jersey, USA.'

'What?' Lexi wasn't sure what to make of it. 'Is it some kind of park, like a theme park? Some old-time-USA theme park? Or a set for a TV show or movie called "Menlo Park"?'

'Or is it actually 1877 and we're in New Jersey?'

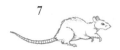

'That's ridiculous.' She pushed the peg away. 'Don't say that's what this is. That's insane.'

'As opposed to the library fogging up and the floor giving way and us falling into a completely bizarre place, dressed in costume?' Al looked above them, in case there was some sign of where they had come from, some sign of the library, but all he could see was the evening sky, clouds and a few birds heading home.

They had fallen and swerved, then fallen again. The fog had pressed in and made Al's ears feel like bursting. His arms and legs had gone numb as the air was forced from his lungs. Then his face had gone numb, the fog had turned black and a humming had started a long way off and grown louder and louder until it was coming at him like a train. Suddenly, they had cleared the cloud and beneath them were islands and a blue sea, and plains that went until the world curved out of sight. Then fields and rivers, roads and buildings, fencelines and houses and a landing no heavier than two falling leaves. In Menlo Park, New Jersey, in 1877.

'Unless we see a teacher soon, I'll Google it,' Lexi said. 'Hey, I think I'm sitting on my phone.' She could feel a bump under her leg among the folds of her skirt and she pulled at them to get to it.

'If it's a movie set, why do all the buildings look real? And where are the cameras?' Al wanted it to be a set, but he wasn't holding out much hope. 'If it's a theme park, where does it end? Where are the rides and the shows and the people trying to sell you stuff?'

'If it's reality TV, you wouldn't see any cameras. It'd look just like the real thing.' Lexi wanted an answer that made 21st century sense.

'A reality TV show that we fell into when the floor of the school library vanished—'

'Look, stop bringing that bit up! I can't deal with it.' She lifted her hand to shield her eyes from the setting sun and stared as far down the road as she could. There was no end to the 19th century in sight. There were no power lines, no aerials or satellite dishes, no planes in the sky. 'It happened when you touched that book.'

She finally found the pocket in her skirt, pulled out her phone and checked the screen.

'No signal.' She pushed a few buttons. 'Not even emergency calls. If this was the 21st century – I so don't want this *not* to be the 21st century. We've got to talk to someone. What do we do? What *can* we do?'

At home she would call. She would call their mother or their father or someone else likely to have an answer, or a car, or money, or whatever it would take. She had an app that should tell her precisely where she was on the planet to within ten metres, but now it told her nothing. She checked some other apps. None of her preferred shops was nearby. None of her friends was nearby. No one was checking in anywhere. She was off the map.

She went to her contacts and scrolled down to their mother's number, but the phone refused to dial it.

She wanted to wake up on a beanbag in the Quiet

Reading area of the library, with a copy of *Anne of Green Gables* or the *Adventures of Huckleberry Finn* or *Little House on the Prairie*. Any reason to be stuck in a dream in 19th century North America would do.

Al stared at the house across the road, wanting it to shake and turn grey and disappear, wanting to fall through a new hole and back into the library, back to lunchtime at Cubberla Creek State School. He told himself it couldn't truly be 1877. They couldn't just leave their own time and end up in the past! But however closely he scrutinised each detail of the world in front of him, he couldn't see one that told him it wasn't 1877.

'Okay, it started with the book in the library and everything else followed that,' he said. 'The book and the pegs must be some kind of kit for something.' But the pegs made no sense by themselves and the book was back in the library. 'We'll find someone. Someone who knows about it. A police officer or someone like that and— ' He had no plan beyond the finding.

'And ask them what century we're in? Say, "Sorry, but we just fell from the sky. Would you mind checking this peg thingy and confirming that that's where we are? And then could we go home? Where can I download an app for that?"'

'You're welcome to have a better idea.' Every time she was negative it sucked a bit more of his hope away. He was used to Lexi having answers, or knowing where to find them. 'That whole closing-your-eyes plan didn't seem to work, and it turns out Mum's not taking calls this century.'

Lexi told herself not to cry. She pulled at her laces. It was then that she noticed Al's books again in his open satchel.

'Why are your books wrapped up? Was that you, or— '

'No. No, that's nothing to do with me. Like the pegs.'

He grabbed the bag and pulled the books out. He turned the package over in his hands. There was an address on the front, and it read, 'Mr Thomas Edison, Edison Laboratories, Menlo Park, New Jersey.'

'Wow, Thomas Edison,' he said. Suddenly the prospect of having fallen into the past looked different. 'Okay. I don't know what's going on, but we've got to go with this. If this really is 1877 and we're really here, we might get to meet Thomas Edison. Maybe the address is a clue. The peg told us where we are, and maybe this will help us find our way back. Maybe we have to get to Edison Laboratories.'

'So, we've fallen into the 19th century,' Lexi said, 'and now you think this Edison guy is going to save us?'

'He's not "this Edison guy", you idiot. He's one of the greatest inventors of the past 500 years. One of the best ever. I can't believe I didn't bring my autograph book.'

'Really? That's what you're worried about, fanboy? We seem to have lost our entire century and you're worried you didn't bring your autograph book?' She shook her head. Al often made her do that. 'You are such a loser.'

'It's not that bad. He'll have paper at the lab. I can use that.'

Lexi groaned. 'Do you really think that was my point? Is this just you getting to tick a surprise box on your history nerd list, or is he actually going to help us?' She did an imaginary

tick in the air. '"Met Thomas Edison. Thought that one was going to be a bit tougher, since he died a million years before I was born, but there you go. And then he sent me back to my own time." Maybe he'll use these pegs.' She picked up a peg again and jiggled the levers around. 'He didn't invent time travel, or we would have seen him on TV talking about it.'

'Still waiting for the better idea, and happy to go with it whenever you're ready.'

Lexi looked up and down the road again. There were no cameras, no theme-park shows and no better ideas. They needed to do something. They would never get home by sitting at the edge of a road, waiting for someone to take them there.

'Okay,' she said. She noticed a man at the next street corner. He was wearing goggles and lifting a long pole up to a streetlight. 'Do we ask that guy poking the light, or is he going to be psycho?'

'Oh, no.' Al worked it out. 'He's not psycho. Not if this is actually 1877. That's what he does. He's a lamplighter. He's exactly the guy we have to ask where Edison Laboratories is! He'll know where things are.'

'Seriously? You think he's lighting it?'

'Er – *"lamplighter"*?'

'So he's not just some crazy guy poking it with a light sabre he made at home? Don't lights just come on when it gets dark?'

'I don't think so,' Al said. 'Not in 1877. I don't know when we got electric streetlights, but gas is what they had then. Or *now*, as it turns out.'

'Don't say that. Don't keep saying it.'

'Lex, we've got to face it. We're in some kind of version of the 19th century and unless everyone we know suddenly jumps out from behind the bushes and yells "surprise", we've got to find our own way out.'

'Yep.' Lexi forced the thought into her head, however much she didn't want to. 'Okay. We've got some sort of

address, we've got the pegs and we're dressed to fit in. Someone planned this. It's some kind of test and we've got to work on the idea that they've given us what we need to pass it. We'll get to the lab and then we'll look for some way of using the pegs. They must be pegs for a reason. And we'll look out for anything along the way – cameras, wiring, anything that doesn't fit in. Any hole we can get through that'll take us back home.' She stood up and shook the street dust from her skirt. 'Okay, it's up to you to pick anything that doesn't fit in. This is your time to shine, history nerd.'

Al could have done without the last bit – he would have preferred the term 'expert' – but he decided to let it go. The rest of it had been exactly what he needed to hear. It sounded like a plan.

The lamplighter was stepping back from the lamp when they arrived at the corner. A blue flame still glowed at the end of his lighting device, which was twice as long as he was tall – and he was unusually tall.

'I have a package to deliver,' Al said, trying to sound like someone on official business in 1877, rather than a twelve-year-old from another century.

'Oh, yes,' the man said, as if he met people like Al all the time. He lifted his goggles and the light of the lamp let him read the address. 'Oh, it's for Mr Edison? You're just two blocks away.' He swung the barrel of his lighter around and pointed to the next side street. 'Two blocks that way. You can't miss it. You'll want the long building – the first one you see from the road.'

'So, this is Menlo Park, New Jersey?' Al said, as if it hadn't been confirmed already. He couldn't find a way of asking if it was 1877. It was hard to know what questions to ask without sounding like they were aliens.

'Every night this week,' the lamplighter said, smiling at his own joke before looking around at the scattered houses and vacant blocks of land. 'It should have been bigger than this by now. There should have been homes everywhere, but that hasn't worked out yet. The Land Company's out of business. Mr Edison's house used to be their office, but his laboratory's a one-off. The biggest sport in Menlo Park is wondering what goes on in there. He's got a carpenter, a blacksmith and a man who does nothing but blow glass. They get some interesting deliveries. I send a few of you folk over that way with packages.' He looked down at the parcel, then smiled again and slid his goggles back down over his eyes. 'They might let you see something in the front room. They do that sometimes. Now, I've got lamps to light or it'll be Menlo Dark, and no one'll thank me for that.'

The smells of cooking came from a house as Lexi and Al walked along the street the lamplighter had indicated. They could hear voices inside. Other than that, and Doug scratching around in the satchel, it was quiet.

'No TVs, no cars,' Al said. Doug scrambled out from under the flap and climbed to his shoulder. 'It feels dead.' Doug's nose pointed in the direction of the dinner smells, but Al wasn't taking the hint.

Al was feeling very stuck in the past at that moment, and a long way from home. Around them, even in this place that hadn't worked out yet as a village, families were being families and getting on with their lives. The sound of a piano playing came from somewhere – probably a house back on the street they had left – and then there were voices singing. Even though he was too far away to understand the words, he could make out the deep voice of a father and the smaller voices of children.

Back home, in the future, in Fig Tree Pocket, he knew his father was planning to cook kun po chicken that night, and he wondered if he would ever get to eat it.

He wanted to still be excited about being in the past, about walking through history when it wasn't a movie or a theme park, about the prospect of meeting Thomas Edison but, at least for a minute or two, he felt too lost for that and – he had to admit it – too scared. If there was no way out, he was a kid in America, born in 1865 and with nowhere to live as night was falling.

A thin black cat followed them to the corner and then darted between the rails of a fence and into long grass. A plate smashed in a house on the other side of the road and a man shouted.

Al told himself he had a puzzle to solve. Lexi said they had been set a test and the only thing to do was to pass it.

Among the new houses and patches of farmland, Edison Laboratories was easy to recognise. It was on a huge block of land, much of which was still open space. Towards the back of it were several small buildings, but the main laboratory was two storeys high and ran most of its length. The gate was open and wheel ruts led in from the road and along the side of the lab.

As Lexi put her hand on the gate, Al stopped.

'I've seen this before,' he said, as he tried to work it out.

'Sure you have.' Lexi kept her hand on the gate, but didn't push it any further. 'Because most lunchtimes you time-travel, right? As if. You've probably just seen a picture.'

'Yeah.' Now that she'd said it, he could almost remember it as a picture, a drawing. He picked Doug up to put him back into the satchel. 'Labs and rats, buddy – not a good combination.' As he closed the satchel again, something caught his eye. 'Hey! The gatepost. It's got my initials on it.'

The writing was in blue pen, an 'A' and an 'H' next to each other. Nearby someone else had written 'JH' and someone had scratched 'TH'.

'But how do we know they're your initials?' Lexi looked around the top of the post for more. 'It's always "something H". There's no "LH", though.'

'It's not always about you.'

She decided to ignore him. 'Can you see any pegs like the ones we've got, or anywhere pegs might go? Or any sign that this has anything to do with the pegs?' She searched up and down the post and tried to move it, but it wouldn't budge.

'Hang on a second.' Al crouched down to check the 'AH' more closely. 'Look at the way the ink's pressed into the wood. It looks like it's from a ballpoint pen.'

'That's a pretty fussy detail you've got there, Sherlock. You were expecting, maybe, a fountain pen?' As she said it, Lexi realised that was exactly what he'd been expecting, and that she was going to have to live through some history nerdishness as Al shared what he knew about the origins of the ballpoint pen. Then she realised what it meant. 'Oh, please tell me there were no ballpoint pens in 1877. Tell me it's wrong and that this is just a pretend 19th century and get us out of here. Or tell me it's wrong and we're not the first to do this – to fall through that stupid wormhole – and then get us out of here.'

'I'm pretty sure the ballpoint pen was the 20th century.' Al scanned the lab complex and its buildings. Nothing else was out of place, as far as he could tell. 'I don't know what it means, but someone from the future seems to have written my initials on this gatepost.'

'Or this whole thing is a fake, a really elaborate fake.' she said. 'Good work. A massive two thumbs up for history nerdishness.'

'We could call it wisdom, okay?' Al said as he walked towards the porch at the end of the long building. 'Let's go and see Mr Edison.'

The front door was already open when they got there, and it led into a room lit by a fat bare light bulb on a wire stand that was set up on a desk.

Al was about to speak when a voice said, 'You're here to see the light, are you?'

A man walked into the room through a doorway behind

the desk. His black hair had a straight part and was slicked into place. 'That's Mr Edison's new filament,' he said, indicating the light bulb. He seemed very proud of it. 'It's platinum. They don't last too long, but look at the quality of the light.'

He looked around the room, which seemed dimly lit to Lexi and Al.

'It'll get better. You'll— ' Al just managed to stop himself suggesting they use carbon instead. He wanted to mention the fishing trip and the split bamboo rod that would give Thomas Edison the idea.

'Um, we're actually here to deliver a package,' Lexi said. 'To Mr Edison.'

'Yes,' Al said, getting back to business. 'The package.'

He opened his satchel and took the wrapped books out. The man looked at the address, and then at Al's jacket and cap.

'Of course,' he said. 'You can leave it with me. I'll see that he gets it.'

He reached out, but Al couldn't let himself hand it over. The parcel might be their only chance of finding a way home. It had to mean something that it was addressed to Thomas Edison himself. Even if it didn't, Al couldn't imagine letting the chance to meet Thomas Edison pass him by.

'Special delivery,' Al said, trying to sound confident. 'Mr Edison has to sign for it.' He hoped they had special deliveries in 1877.

For a moment the man looked as if he was going to argue, but then he shrugged. 'All right, but I'll have to take you there myself. Follow me.'

He led them through the doorway, into a long hall lit by gas lamps. Behind closed doors on either side, they could hear the noises of machines – the hums and hisses and grinding and clanging, and the fizz of static that said inventors were at work. Behind one door, Al thought he could hear someone saying, 'Mary had a little lamb' slowly and clearly, over and over. He tried to get Lexi's attention, but she was looking straight ahead.

At the far end of the hall was a large room that looked like a laboratory and, just inside it, the man stopped. 'You can wait here,' he said. 'I'll see if Mr Edison's available. Please touch nothing, and please do not leave this room.'

He stepped back into the hall and knocked on the second door along. A whirring sound stopped, and the door opened.

A voice said, 'Yes?'

The man stuck his head around the door and spoke too quietly for Lexi and Al to hear.

'I think we just heard the invention of the phonograph,' Al whispered, about to go into a lot of detail. 'Mary had a little—'

Lexi held her hand up. 'I think I want to live in the 21st century. Focus. You can tell me about the phony-whatever later, if you have to. Is anything historically wrong in this room? Anything like the ballpoint pen? Or do you see anything that goes with the pegs?'

There was a gas lamp on a nearby table, with a knob on its base. Al reached out and turned it, and the light became brighter.

The room had tables covered with pipes, blown glass and gadgets. There were bookcases along one wall, and below a window was a cabinet with lockable drawers. Al signalled to Lexi to keep watching the hallway and he moved over to it as quietly as he could and tried to open one of the drawers. It stayed shut. He wondered where the key might be. He took the glowing Menlo Park peg from his bag and tried its key in the lock, but it didn't fit. It was clear the others wouldn't either.

The voices from the other room were louder now.

'But, Mr Edison, Alexander Graham Bell's already started using "ahoy" to answer the telephone,' someone said. 'We all agree we need to make up some kind of greeting, and it's a simple enough word.'

'Bell has only two sets of telephones, one connected to the other, and they're on either side of a thin wall.' The voice must have been Thomas Edison's. 'He hasn't run a line across the country. Bell doesn't own this. He's welcome to shout "ahoy" at people if he wants to, but he can't tell the rest of us to do that. He might have invented the receiver, but the microphone is mine and I shall be saying "hello" into it.'

'Mr Edison,' the man who had brought them to the room said politely, but a little louder than before. 'I don't mean to interrupt— '

At that moment, Lexi noticed something. The bottom right-hand corner of a painting on the wall seemed to be glowing in the lamplight. The painting was of a ship, with a whale rising from the water next to it.

She went over to investigate exactly where the glow was coming from. What she saw made her call out to Al. In the corner of the painting, where the artist's signature would have been, was a button with '& more' written on it. It was pulsing with a golden light.

'I think this is it,' she said. 'This is our way out. It's like the one in the dictionary.'

'But I haven't met Mr Edison yet.'

'I don't care if it's the real 19th century or not. I'm not getting stuck here just because you want to meet someone from your Great Nerds of History team.' Lexi touched the button. 'I want to go home.'

A hole opened up, with a golden rim. It was the size of a pencil, then a finger and then, Al realised, exactly the size of the peg that he was holding in his hand and that was starting to hum.

'Okay,' he said. 'At least I heard him. Hearing Thomas Edison talk about the phone is nearly— '

Lexi snatched the peg from him, lifted it up to the hole and slid it inside. It clicked neatly into place. Al pulled the levers down to hold it there.

The voices along the hall turned fuzzy and then quiet. The lamplight grew dim. The room started to shudder.

Al turned the key in the end of the peg.

The floor dropped away and they were falling again.

1835

Off the coast
of Nantucket
USA

MAGNOVIEW

$\mathcal{T}$HIS TIME THEY dropped straight down. Al shut his eyes and told himself not to scream like a baby.

Then he screamed like a baby.

Lexi stuck her arms out to the side and it steadied her. Pressure was building in her ears and her lungs. She looked down, but there was nothing to see.

With a jolt, the air cleared. She could breathe and, far below, dawn was coming to the world. The sun gleamed from a thick fog bank over the ocean and lit the edge of the land. There were forests, and a peninsula the shape of a hook. It wasn't home. It wasn't even Australia. Whatever they were falling towards, it wasn't the library at Cubberla Creek State School.

'Al!' she shouted.

Al stopped screaming and opened his eyes. What he saw made him take a big breath in, and he only just managed not to turn it into a new scream on the way out. This time, they were heading for the water.

They fell faster and faster, punched through the top of the fog bank and suddenly their fall became a drift and they landed lightly on the cold wet timber deck of a ship.

Al opened his hand and saw a red mark where the key from 1877 had pressed into his palm. The fog was thick around them and it wasn't easy to make out shapes. They were sheltered by the hull of a smaller boat that seemed to be suspended above the deck on posts, ready for launching. Across the deck, Al could see the base of a black mast and the bottom part of a taut wet sail almost the colour of fog.

'This isn't home,' Lexi said.

Al looked at her. She had a large leather hat on that was wet with sea spray, and a leather coat. So did he. 'What was your first clue?' he said.

This time was almost worse. The first fall had taken them away from their own time and he had wanted the second one to be its exact reverse and take them back. So much for that idea.

The ship lifted as a wave passed under it and then dropped again. Al always got sick at sea.

'Thomas Edison said "Hello".' Lexi sounded better than Al felt. 'And then the button on the picture started glowing. And it was "Hello" in the dictionary that had that glowing button you pressed. Do you think— '

'Hello,' Al said, trying not to vomit. 'Hello.'

Nothing happened. Nothing glowed. Saying 'Hello' wasn't an easy way out.

'Stop looking down,' Lexi told him. 'Look straight ahead. Look at – okay, there's no horizon. Just look straight ahead.'

The ship climbed again, then dropped. Al felt totally out of sync with his stomach, as if someone had attached it to a bungee cord and let go.

'Maybe it needs someone other than us to say "Hello",' Lexi said, before realising that Al had stopped paying attention. 'You probably don't need to do that screaming if we have another one of those falls. It looks like they're not fatal.'

'I wasn't screaming.' Al thought he could hear Doug throwing up in his bag. Doug had never been good with motion either. 'It was just how the air came out of me.'

'Yep,' Lexi said. 'Think I remember that excuse from the Tower of Terror at Dreamworld.' She wanted to be the strong one. She wanted them both to be strong and for Al not to throw up. 'Okay, we've proved we can get somewhere. We know how to do this.' She wanted to believe it as well as say it. They had made it out of 1877, or at least out of New Jersey.

Al's bag was now a canvas duffel bag and he pulled open the string at the top. This time, the glow inside wasn't a surprise. As he reached for the peg, his hand struck a slick of rat vomit. Doug scuttled halfway up his arm and sat picking a tiny chunk of carrot from between his teeth with a claw.

'Oh no,' Al managed to say, as his morning tea surged out of his stomach and splattered onto the deck. 'Aargh. Vomit always makes me vomit.' He kept his face over the spot in case there was more to come. He took a few deep breaths and tried not to look at the pulverised apple and chewed muesli bar.

'You think I don't know that? Honestly, all that water out there and you have to do it on the deck right next to me.' Lexi had had a lifetime of Al's vomiting.

She opened the neck of the bag wider, so that she could see the peg before reaching for it. Unfortunately, it was sitting in Doug's vomit. She lifted it out with two fingers then scraped the vomit out of the bag with the edge of one of Al's schoolbooks.

'Don't say I never do anything for you,' she said, as she wiped the book on the deck and tried to ignore the smell of both human and rat vomit. 'There's still two more pegs in there. Does that mean we have to do this three more times?' She looked up in case she could see the sky, or something, but there was only fog. 'There's never been any sign of a way back.' She checked the peg she was holding. '1835.' She tried to show it to Al, but he didn't want to read it.

'We've gone *back* in time?' Al felt another wave of nausea and kept staring at the deck. 'Further back?'

'Or just to a different – whatever this is. This is just a wooden ship.' She wanted it to be part of a test, a puzzle. 'But just because the peg says 1835 –'

'What if none of them takes us home? What if they take us further and further back and the last one drops us off on a volcano 50 million years ago and we're surrounded by raptors?'

'Raptors who had some connection with the word "hello"?' Lexi wanted it to sound as absurd as she could make it. She wanted it to be impossible. 'It was probably their word for meat. Fresh meat.' She held the peg in front of him again. 'Have you ever heard of Nantucket?'

Al didn't answer right away. He went to put the key from 1877 in his pocket, but his hand just slid down the wet coat. He tucked it into his shoe instead. He didn't know if he would ever need the key again, but it seemed smarter to keep it, just in case. He put his hands onto the deck to steady himself, and tried to focus on the bow, which he could just make out through the haze.

'Um, I don't know.' At least 1835 was something for him to concentrate on. 'Victoria's nearly queen, but not quite. Charles Darwin might have started the trip on the *Beagle* that led to the theory of evolution.' The ship dropped again, and Al passed his stomach on the way down. 'That's it. That's all I've got.'

'Charles Darwin didn't come here, though, did he?' She said it as if it wasn't really a question. 'Isn't there someone in 1835 who you're busting to meet?' No answer. 'Okay, so what do we do now?'

'We go on,' Al said. 'There's no choice. I either lose more morning tea or I don't, but, whatever, we've got to find another hole, put another peg in it and hope it's the one that takes us home.'

At the bow of the ship, Al could just make out a man with a megaphone. He was next to something that looked like a gun mounted on the deck. Al watched the man lift the megaphone to his mouth and shout 'Halloo' out into the fog.

The ship rolled and pitched in the heavy sea, but the man at the bow was steady on his feet. Al tried to stand, but fell over before he was halfway up.

From somewhere in the distance, perhaps directly in front of the ship, a voice came back shouting, 'Halloo!'

'Oh, no,' Al said, to himself as much as anything. 'I thought the first guy said "Hello". I thought that could be it.'

'Maybe it was. Maybe it's close enough.' Lexi grabbed his elbow and pulled him to his feet. 'Hey – this might be

where Mister Edison got it from – from "halloo".' Al still looked unsteady. 'Lean against the boat, the little boat.'

Lexi looked around for a glow, or anywhere to put the peg, but there was nothing. The fog had closed in again on all sides and the deck was just dark wet wood.

'Give way to starboard,' a voice called out from behind them and above their heads.

There was a wheelhouse on a raised deck, and they could make out two men in it. One had given the order and the other was turning the wheel. A whistle sounded and the ship started to change direction. Ahead of them in the fog, another whistle signalled back.

'Flotsam off the starboard bow, captain,' the man with the megaphone shouted.

Up in the wheelhouse, the captain called out, 'All hands to the starboard bow. All hands to the starboard bow. Prepare to salvage flotsam at the starboard bow.'

As two men ran past Lexi and Al, one shouted out, 'Get moving! The captain called for all hands.'

The men were dressed just like Lexi and Al, and the broad brims of their hats hung low with the weight of sea spray and rain. There was no way to see their faces, or for them to see Lexi and Al properly.

'They think we're crew,' Lexi said, peering ahead to see what was happening. 'Come on. I think we should go.'

Al felt better standing, or at least less awful. His knees could absorb some of the up-and-down motion. With one hand each on the small boat to steady them, they made their way forward.

'Hey,' Lexi said, 'initials again. "AH", "TH".' They were marked on the deck, one scratched into the wood, the other written in ink. It felt good to see them there. Lexi couldn't say why, but it made her feel less lost.

As they reached another mast, they could see the crew at work, maybe eight men leaning over the side with hooks to pull something heavy on board. As it rose from the water, Lexi and Al could see it was a timber packing crate, crusted with barnacles and weed.

The ship dropped from the crest of a wave and they ran over to help. They braced themselves just as the crew were doing, and they reached out to the crate. It was slippery, but they could just get their hands around the side of it to help pull it on board.

'It's heavy,' one of the crew said. 'Do you think it could be gold or silver?'

'It's floating,' a deeper voice said from the other end of the crate. 'It's not that heavy. I don't think we're all going to go home rich, Jack. All together now. Pull.'

The crate lifted, then tilted over the edge and fell onto the deck.

'Ship to port!' the man with the megaphone shouted as the dark bow of another whaler loomed out of the fog. 'Forty yards and closing. Crew to port.'

The other crew members crossed to the port side of the ship, leaving Lexi and Al with the crate on the deck. The second whaler tilted to come down a wave, throwing up spray from its bow. If the next wave hit at the wrong angle, the two ships would come together. If the crews couldn't keep them apart, both could end up wrecked in this rough, dark sea.

Then Lexi noticed something on the side of the crate. There was a murky glow in just one spot. She scraped away the weed covering it, and '& more' shone at her from a golden 'O' in the word 'venison'.

'Twenty yards and closing,' the bow man said. The wheelhouse of the other whaler was now visible through the fog. 'We're two yards clear if we can both hold course.'

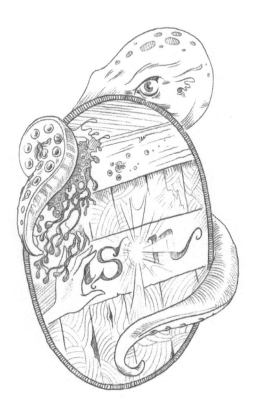

Lexi pushed the 'O' and it fell back into the wood, leaving a hole with a golden rim.

The ship lurched up the face of another wave and Al stumbled. He dropped his bag and it skidded across the deck. He crawled after it and fell on it as they rode over the crest of the wave. He reached inside for the glowing peg.

'Come on,' Lexi shouted. 'It's opening already.'

The crate was buzzing as the hole grew wider and brighter. The peg in Al's hand started to hum as he came closer.

The ship hit the next wave and spray shot over them. Al grabbed onto the crate with one hand as he lost his footing again. With his other hand, he drove the peg into the hole and gold light flared across the deck.

As Lexi reached across to lock the levers down, they heard a voice from the other ship – a man shouting, 'No!'

Al was already turning the key as they looked around. The deck was shuddering, the sea had turned to foam and, as they started falling, the last thing they saw from the other ship was a flash of gold through the fog.

1100
the
New Forest
England

MAGNOVIEW

ERHAPS IT WAS the wind that did it, though it didn't feel like it. Something made them veer sideways as they fell, again in gathering darkness. With a lurch they slowed down, but kept falling. Then they hit a bump – or some change in the air that felt like a bump – followed by sustained turbulence. Then they swerved, as if they were dodging something, before a downdraft flung them clear and into daylight over a forest that went on and on.

Al did all he could to keep his mouth shut and then discovered it was humanly possible to do a kind of scream through his nose.

They landed in a clearing.

Al cleared his throat and pretended the scream had come from someone else. He leant back against a fallen tree trunk. His stomach was back in his body again.

He was wearing leggings that laced together at the waist and a rough shirt that went most of the way down to his knees. Lexi was wearing the same. That hardly seemed fair, since Lexi was happy to wear leggings back in real life. This version of the past looked a lot better on her than it did on him.

'Yuk,' she said, running her hands through her matted hair, or trying to. 'I don't think I've washed my hair for about a hundred years.'

Al touched his head. Once, on a camping trip, he had tested how long he could go without washing his hair, but had cracked after five days. His new hair felt far worse. He tried not to imagine the small animals that might be living in it. At least the motion had stopped. In the sack on his shoulder, he heard Doug sigh. He had never heard a rat sigh before.

'We're nowhere near home, are we?' Lexi said. 'We're dressed nothing like home. Give me the bad news.'

Al put the sack on the ground and undid the cord that was keeping it closed. He could see Doug's fur glowing in the light from the peg.

'1100,' he said, as he showed Lexi the peg. He tried to imagine it before it came properly to life in front of them. He wondered what was next.

The sun was high above them, the day was warm and there were bees buzzing around the flowers in the clearing. He tucked the peg into his rope belt and put his sack down on the grass. He could hear Doug sniffing the forest's smells – tiny flowers, honey, damp earth, fungus, smoke from a wood fire, poo, yes, more poo. The poo of quite a big animal, maybe; a grass-eating animal.

'So, somewhere in this forest, someone's going to say something about "hello" and then there'll be another one of those button things, whatever they are,' Lexi said. 'Except we need a better name for them than "button things". Something right for time travel, or whatever this is. What about "portal"?'

'Yeah. Very *Doctor Who.*' *Doctor Who* was the one TV show the whole family was into. 'I like it. Portal.'

They had reverse dinner every *Doctor Who* night, starting with dessert. Their father had been a fan since he was about six, when he had hidden behind the sofa with the dogs any time the daleks came out. He had always raved about the early *Doctor Who* and bought the DVD box set as soon as it was released. It was in black and white, and most of the props looked as if they had been built from scraps lying around the studio. Al could remember their father explaining that, before CGI and back in the days of imagination, props like that could still be pretty scary.

Because of *Doctor Who*, they had talked about travelling through time and where they would go and what they would want to see, but the style of time travel discussed over dinner was always smoother and easier. Al picked great moments in history and imagined watching them from a safe distance and being in control. He didn't once pick vomiting in fog.

'What's not to like about 1100 so far?' he said. 'Other than the lack of shampoo. What do you think we're looking for?'

'Oh, because I made up the rules for this?' Lexi was picking something sticky from her hair. 'Anything to do with "Hello". A portal. That's all I've got. Same as you.' She wiped her hand on the ground and reached down to tighten the laces on her boots, which were very worn and seemed to be different sizes. 'I think I robbed two different people for these. What are we supposed to be?'

43

'Well, we're in a forest, and I think regular people avoided forests in 1100.' Al checked his shoes. They were worse than Lexi's. 'It's the kind of place where outlaws went to hide.'

'Like Robin Hood? People like that?'

'And a lot of people not like that.' History, real history, didn't have so many merry men in forests. 'But we should be okay. We don't look like we've got anything worth stealing.' Something on a tree at the edge of the clearing caught his eye. 'Hey, what's that?'

It looked like writing. He stood up and moved a branch aside so that he could read it clearly. 'TH' had been scratched into the bark. Further down, he found an 'A' and the start of another 'H'.

'We're still on track.' He didn't know what track that might be, but the other 'H's had been here. He told himself it meant they weren't completely lost.

'And look down at the bottom of the tree – I think there's money.' Lexi bent down and picked up a silver coin. 'It looks like an old coin, except it's brand new.'

She handed it to Al, who turned it over and looked at it closely.

'It's newer than new. It's from the future. See this bit here?' He pointed to some letters. '"Elizab" and then "Regi". That's Queen Elizabeth. Elizabeth the first. She's queen 500 years from now. "DG" means "dei gratia", "by the grace of God", the "Ang" is England, the "Hib" is Ireland, which was once Hibernia.' Sometimes great facts burst out of him, before he could manage to hold them back.

44

Lexi laughed. 'The freak is back – long live the freak.'

They went down on their knees to look for more coins, but there didn't seem to be any.

'It's the ballpoint pen all over again, isn't it?' Al said. 'We're not the first people here from the future. The "H" people are from the future, like us.'

'And maybe they got home,' Lexi said, as she stood up. 'They're not here now. Maybe they knew what they were doing.' She looked around, but all she could see were trees. 'Or maybe they stumbled through and made it anyway.'

A clanging sound came from somewhere in the forest behind them, and a man's voice shouted. He sounded annoyed. Someone else laughed.

'Maybe they went that way,' Lexi said, as she turned to look. 'The "H"s. Should we try to find whoever's over there?'

'I don't know.' There was silence in the forest again. Al tried to remember the exact sounds he had heard. 'One of them laughed. That suggests they don't mind if people hear them. It all sounded okay, like someone making a mess of something on a camping trip.' Outlaws would be quiet, he thought. They wouldn't want to be found. It might be men who had come to cut timber, or catch game for the lord of the manor. 'We can't just sit here. Let's go, but let's be careful.'

They made the best guess they could about where the noise had come from, and they left the clearing. Al wanted a compass and a map. Better shoes, bottled water, their father. He stopped making a list of the things he wanted. They were all 900 years away, and he and Lexi weren't bushwalking in a national park close to home.

They climbed a low hill and scrambled down the other side. At the top of the next hill, Lexi held out her hand to stop him.

'Listen,' she said quietly.

If they stayed completely still, they could hear men talking and a rhythmic rasping sound. Doug's head poked from Al's bag. His nose was twitching.

'Food,' Al whispered. 'They're making food. Someone's sharpening a knife, or sharpening something.'

As they moved further through the trees, they could see more light ahead, another clearing. The smell of smoke grew stronger. A building took shape among the trees. It was made of forest timber and had a thatched roof. Lexi stopped and looked at Al.

'It's a hunting lodge, I think,' he whispered. 'Probably for the lord of the manor, or whoever owns the forest. The thatch for the roof would have been brought in from a town. It looks too good to be an outlaw's place.'

'Great. We should be all right then.' Lexi started walking again. 'Maybe they're the people we need to find. We'll go up to them, they'll say some version of "hello" and away we go.'

'I don't know if it'll be that easy, but, yeah. Maybe.' Al hoped she was right. The forest seemed to go on forever and the men ahead seemed like the only other people in it.

At the back of the building was a table with two big round cheeses, loaves of bread, a sack of herbs and an open wooden chest with goblets in it made of a dull metal. Doug pushed his way to the top of Al's sack again, and Al pushed him back down.

The men's voices were clearer now.

'I know they're most likely to come back with boar,' one of them said, 'but I've got to be ready to cook whatever they've got. It might be pheasant, and that's completely different cooking. It might be anything. All you've got to do is be ready to cut it up.'

While Al concentrated on the conversation, Lexi picked up a goblet and felt the weight of it in her hands. There were pictures of bunches of grapes stamped into the metal. She and Al had once gone on a school excursion to see an old play in a park, and the actors had used goblets that looked almost the same.

'Lexi, I—' Al was about to suggest that she put it down when one of the men came around the corner.

The man stopped. He was thin and bent over, and he had a scar on his face. He looked at Lexi holding the goblet, and at Al, and at the forest behind them. He reached for his belt, but there was nothing there for his hand to take.

'Thieves!' he shouted. 'We've got thieves, Gilbert!'

'No, I—' Lexi wanted to tell him about the play, and that she'd only been looking at the goblet, but he was already lunging towards her.

She threw the goblet and he stopped to catch it before it hit the ground.

'Lex, run!' Al shouted, grabbing her arm and pulling her away.

The man chased after them. Al passed to the right of the first tree and Lexi to the left. Al's sack snagged on something, but he pulled it free and ran on. He dodged another tree, jumped a log and scrambled through a bush and up a hill. He skidded as he ran down the other side of it, but he stayed on his feet and kept running.

He was sure he had Lexi right behind him all the way, but, at the top of the next hill, he checked for the first time. She wasn't there.

Further back through the trees, he heard a scream.

Lexi was caught. She twisted and tried to scratch, but the man pinned her arms to her sides.

He had tackled her and winded her, but she had got up

and tried to fight him off. He was behind her now, with his arms around her.

Screaming was the first thing to do. That's what she'd learned in the women's self-defence classes she'd taken with her mother in the school hall. She tried to focus, to remember more. She tried not to panic.

She lifted her right foot and ground the heel of her boot into his shin. She scraped it down the bone and then stamped hard on his foot. He shouted and, for a second, loosened his grip. She drove her right elbow under his ribs with all the force she could manage. She heard the breath wheeze out of him as he fell backwards.

She ran. Straight ahead and then right and then left. She could hear him back through the trees, stumbling around. She picked up a stick and kept running. She reached the top of a hill and half-ran half-fell down the other side.

Just when she thought she was safe, she heard someone coming at her across the fallen leaves to her right.

She turned to run to the left, and then heard Al say, 'Lex, it's me.'

She stopped. He had a stick in his hand, too.

'Keep going,' he said, checking the hill behind her. 'I think we're okay.'

He let her lead this time and kept looking over his shoulder. Once they were just over the next slope, he caught up with Lexi and signalled for her to stop. They crouched down and looked back through the forest. There was no one there, and not a sound that could be heard over the wind in the trees.

Lexi took her hand from her stick and stretched her fingers.

'He caught me,' she said. 'That guy. I don't know what he was going to do. Do they have police in 1100?'

'Not really.' Al didn't know what the man would have done either, but he guessed it wouldn't have been good. Things didn't tend to go so well for people stealing goblets. 'We've got to be careful. You can probably just walk up to people in 1877, but not in 1100. Not in a forest, looking like an outlaw. Particularly not when you pick up their stuff.'

'Oh, right, so this is all my fault?' She kept her voice down, but only just. 'I can't believe you left me. Ran away and left me.'

'I didn't. I thought we were running together. And I came back.'

At home, she would have fought him about it. And over who got the last Tim Tam, who got control of the TV remote, who used up all the monthly download allocation, whose turn it was to do one stupid chore or another.

Her heart was still racing. Inside she was still running, still fighting the man who had grabbed her. She felt strong and ready and dizzy, all at the same time. The stick was in her hands again. Al had come back for her, she knew he had.

'That's the last time we ever split up until we get home, okay?' she said.

'Definitely.' A bird flew past, and Al noticed Lexi flinch. 'I heard that guy screaming. I don't know what you did to him, but it must have been pretty nasty.'

'Turns out having boots with ugly wooden heels isn't all bad.' Lexi smiled. 'Let's go.'

They kept moving, to put more distance between themselves and the hunting lodge.

Once they were safe, Al started to feel lost again. There was a portal set to open somewhere, but all they had around them was forest. He could find the sun through the tree canopy, but he couldn't remember how to use it to navigate. And he had no idea where they had to go.

'Hey,' Lexi said, pointing across the clearing they'd just walked into. 'That tree. We're back where we started. Maybe the coin and the writing on the tree meant we should have stayed here.'

'That could be the best idea we've had all century.'

Al sat down on the log that had fallen at the edge of the clearing, and Lexi looked around to see if any other trees had writing on them.

'So, 1100 in the New Forest,' she said, 'and there's a hunting trip on somewhere around here. What happens? Any ideas?'

Suddenly, Al remembered. 'Oh, no. I can think of one thing … '

There was a noise in the trees to one side of the clearing, hooves thumping on the forest floor, undergrowth being flattened or beaten aside. Three deer appeared, moving at high speed. They ducked sideways when they saw Lexi and Al, but they didn't slow down. They were through the clearing and back into the forest in a few bounds. A horse

charged out of the trees in pursuit, and the rider pulled hard on its reins to stop it. They were both breathing heavily.

He looked down from his saddle at Lexi and Al. He had a broad chest and wavy golden hair, and his face was flushed.

'And who are you,' he said, 'to be here in the king's forest?'

He was looking at Lexi, glaring at her. She told herself she'd done nothing wrong. There was no goblet this time, no reason to call her a thief.

'We're just—' She tried to sound calm, even though she didn't feel it. 'I'm sure the king won't mind. We're trying to get home.'

'What?' The rider didn't like the answer at all. 'Who are you to read the mind of the king?'

'We don't mean any trouble,' Al said. The man had a bow, a quiver full of arrows on his back and a knife in a sheath on his belt. Al tried to picture King William II. William Rufus. He had always thought he had red hair. 'We're not outlaws. Our father's a stonemason. He builds churches. We're lost.'

'Oh, really?' he said. 'Lost? Lost and with the king's catch in that sack of yours? What have you got there? Partridges? A hare?'

From behind the rider there was more noise in the forest, another pursuit. Two more deer ran into the clearing. They jumped either side of his horse and kept their heads down as they reached the trees on the other side.

A call went up, a man's voice shouting, 'Harrow! Harrow!'

'Your Majesty,' Al said, taking a guess. 'If you are actually the king, you need to move now.'

The rider turned in his saddle.

'Lex.' Al grabbed her arm. 'We have to go.'

'But "harrow"?' She shook his arm free. 'Maybe that's the clue – the next step after "halloo". Or before it.'

'Clue?' The rider moved to face them again. 'And what do you— '

Lexi and Al didn't even see the arrow that came through the trees and struck him in the back. It hit with a thump, like a fist, and the rider slumped forward. Half the shaft of the arrow stuck out of his tunic, with feathers cut in a neat V-shape at the end of it, each one dyed red and with a gold lion painted on it.

'That's it,' Al said. 'That's what happens in the New Forest in 1100. And he's the king.'

'Harrow!' the voice shouted again, as three men on horses burst through the trees with bows drawn.

They pulled their horses up hard, and one horse lifted its front legs and almost threw its rider.

They stared at the king, who was still in his saddle, his face almost touching his horse's mane. He wasn't moving. His horse lifted a hoof, scuffed the ground and shook its head. The reins were still in the king's hands.

'My Lord,' one of the riders said to the man on the leading horse. 'The king is shot. The king is dead.'

'No!' the man said desperately. He was older than the other two, and wore a dagger with a jewelled hilt. He dropped

his bow and jumped down from his horse. He looked pale, panicked. 'He can't be. He was beside us a moment ago. But the arrow – it's the arrow he gave me. I can't deny it. One of the two he gave me from his own quiver last night after we ate. He did it in front of a dozen barons. "To the good archer, the good arrows." Now this.'

He ran over and took the reins of the king's horse. The horse stepped back and pulled its head away. The king slid from the saddle and fell. He hit the ground with a thump and lay face down in the grass. The king was dead, all right. There was no doubt about it.

Lexi and Al started backing away. The shooting of a king in a forest seemed a bad thing to have witnessed, far worse than touching a goblet. But if 'harrow' was the word, where was the portal? And how long would it last?

One of the younger riders dismounted, went over to the king's body and knelt down. He grabbed the arrow below the feathers and snapped it off at the point where it stuck out of the king's back. He stood up again and threw the piece of arrow into the trees.

'Not your arrow, my Lord,' he said to the older man, who seemed to be stuck to the spot where he was standing. 'Not the king's good arrow. It was some rough outlaw's arrow that killed him. So rough that it broke when it went in.'

He turned to Lexi and Al.

'Yes,' the older man said. 'Yes, Richard, you're right.' He looked at the other man, who nodded. 'I, Walter Tyrell, Lord of Poix and of Langham, baron in the loyal service of William II, King of England, arrest you for the king's murder. You will be taken immediately from this place to Winchester and to justice.'

'Harrow,' Al said to Lexi. He felt sick. 'Where is it?'

Lexi looked around desperately. Sunlight glinted from the men's gold belt buckles, and from the dagger one of them had drawn, but she couldn't see a portal.

'Fix the king upon his horse, Richard,' Walter Tyrell said. 'Close his eyes and his mouth and tie him in his saddle for now. We'll find a cart and dress it well and take him to Winchester with dignity.'

'It's daylight,' Lexi said to Al. Her mouth was dry and she felt dizzy. 'It's probably glowing already. We just can't see it.'

'What are you talking about?' Walter Tyrell was looking at her. He seemed uneasy. 'What's glowing? Are you a witch, girl? Did you bend my arrow in its flight and send it into the body of the king?'

At that moment, the man called Richard tried to lift the king, and the king's body rolled over. Arrows slipped from the quiver that had been by his side – four arrows with markings identical to the one that had struck him. The quiver came to rest on top of the king's body, and on the bottom of it was a glowing gold button with '& more' on it.

'Yes,' Lexi said to Walter Tyrell. Her voice shook, but she told herself to sound strong, fearless. 'I am a witch. I can bend the flight of arrows. I can send them from the ground to a man's chest or his face. Step back, my Lord. I don't like your face at all.' She pointed to the king's fallen arrows. 'Rise, arrows, on my command. Rise and strike –' She stuck her other hand out, pointing straight at Walter Tyrell – 'this awful man.'

Al grabbed the peg from his belt and held it up with both hands, like something magical.

'Step back,' he told Richard. 'Step back, every one of you, or she'll kill you all.'

Richard scrambled away from the king's body. Lexi and Al moved towards King William and knelt down on the ground. Lexi touched the portal and it opened. The peg shook in Al's hand as he drove it in.

'What is this?' the one man still on his horse said, as Al pulled the levers down. 'I've seen no witchcraft. I see two thieves in the king's forest. Two murderers.'

He slid an arrow from his quiver and put it to his bow. As he drew it back and took aim, Al turned the key.

The arrow blurred, the rider blurred, mist took Walter Tyrell and the fallen king, and the ground fell away.

925

Outside Rouen
Normandy
France

MAGNOVIEW

$\mathcal{T}$HERE WAS A shudder, and Lexi and Al were flung sideways. They fell into darkness – close, damp darkness – and then out of it, into fresh air above another forest. There was a town in the distance, with stone and timber buildings and thatched roofs, but they barely glimpsed it before it disappeared from view.

Just above tree height, they slowed down and Al felt the blood rush back into his face. They dropped through the branches to the forest floor, landing on dry leaves that had fallen the previous autumn.

Up through the tree canopy, the sky was a vivid blue. They looked around to all sides and listened. There was wind in the trees, but no sound other than that.

'Different forest,' Lexi said. 'No Walter Tyrell.' Her heart was still pounding, so hard she could almost hear it.

'Hello' had come a long way from a harmless greeting. Lexi found herself turning to check behind her. She listened for hooves, voices, anything. She wanted to be ready.

'Nice work with that witch thing,' Al said. He steadied himself and waited for the dizziness to pass. 'Good to see you're getting something out of all that trash TV.'

'No problem. We can't rely on your old books for everything. People in history totally freaked about witches, didn't they?' She could feel her legs shaking. She wasn't ready to stand yet. 'And that Walter guy – he'd just shot the king, and that'd make you pretty edgy. Is it true? Was that real?'

'I'm not sure.' There were leaves in Al's hair and he shook them out. 'King William did get killed on a hunting trip in the New Forest in 1100, but I don't know the details. I'm not sure anyone does.'

Lexi noticed she was wearing a dress that went down to her ankles, and an embroidered tunic.

'I think we're richer this time,' she said. 'Our clothes are fancier. You're still wearing that weird kind of lace-up pants thing, though. They're very fitted. You've so got the legs of a chicken.'

'I—' Al looked down at his legs. It would have been better if the fabric hadn't been yellow. What a loser. 'Great. I look like a bird people would hunt. I'm just waiting for someone to shout "harrow", and for the madness to start again.'

His bag was made of finer cloth this time, with an embroidered shoulder strap. This time they weren't outlaws. No one would think they'd turned up to steal things.

'This is the last one,' he said, as he took out the glowing peg.

They read it together.

'We're in France? In a year that doesn't even have four digits? 925? Every time, we're further from home. And this is it, our last shot.' Lexi turned the peg over so she didn't have to keep looking at the writing. 'This thing – whatever it

is – is a total nightmare in English. How are we going to get through it when everyone's speaking French?'

'Mum speaks French.' As soon as he had said it, Al wished he hadn't.

'Yeah. So, if you can get us about a thousand years closer to a good mobile signal, maybe we can call her.' Lexi didn't want to think about it either. She had never imagined being quite so far from anything or anyone she knew. 'What's next? What are we up for?'

'I don't know. I don't do Normandy. Not until next century, anyway.' He stood up. He tried to remember when the Normans arrived in northwest France. 'But, hey, now I know about William II. Like, really *know*. And I can go back home and—'

He wanted to tell people. He wanted to write history, accurately, as its witness. It was Walter Tyrell who had fired the shot, and Al himself had seen the arrow hit. But straightaway he knew it wouldn't work, not from a twelve-year-old in the 21st century. He wanted evidence – the arrow, something – but even that wouldn't prove to anyone in the future that he was there at the time.

He looked around for initials – 'AH', 'TH' and the rest – but couldn't see any. It was dark in the forest, and anything on the ground was covered in leaves. He hoped the others had been there, whoever they were. And he hoped they had made it home.

'Did you see a road?' Lexi said. 'I'm pretty sure there's a road over that way.'

She pointed through the trees. Al hadn't seen it.

'Yeah,' he said. His eyes had been closed most of the time while they fell. He told himself it was because of the wind, the cold air at that altitude. At least he had put the screaming behind him. 'Let's try it. If the peg says "outside Rouen", maybe we should find the road and go that way.'

Lexi led the way among the trees. They could see more of the sky as they approached the road, and then the road itself was in front of them. It was nothing more than cleared dirt, rutted by wheels. To the left, they could see it until it rose to the top of a low hill and then dipped down the other side. To the right, it curved out of sight into the forest. Directly in front of them, on the other side of the road, were a large boulder and several smaller rocks. The forest was less dense on that side, with the trees growing around rocky outcrops.

'So,' Lexi said, 'you think we go to Rouen, which must be the town that way?' She pointed to the left.

'I just thought if we needed to hear something about "hello", we should go where there are more people.' As soon as he said it, Al was less sure of it. 'Except we're already back to "harrow", and that seems to be something you shout in a forest, and that means danger or get out of the way. Maybe we should try different directions.'

'Yeah, maybe. But only if we do it together. We're not splitting up again. Not if people are going to start attacking us. Which they will. We're in a forest in the olden days, waiting for a word that means danger.' At school, Lexi was always happy when the class divided into groups and she and Al weren't put together. But school was more than a thousand years away, and nothing like the past.

'I don't mean splitting up. I don't want that either.' He wasn't going to forget Lexi's scream in the New Forest, and how scared and powerless he had felt. 'Anyway, what if we were separated when one of us found the portal? We can't split up. But we haven't seen any initials or signs that we've landed where we should. How about we keep each other in sight, but just walk in different directions down the road, looking for any kind of clue?'

'A button,' Lexi said, with a certainty Al wasn't expecting.

'It's a bit early to get that lucky. Someone would have to say something first. We're not just going to walk up to a portal.'

'No, not an "& more" button.' Lexi was pointing down at the ground. 'A regular button.'

She walked past him and bent down to pick it up.

'I'm trying to think if they had buttons—'

'It's plastic.' She wiped it on her sleeve and showed it to him. 'Looks like 1960s. Or '50s.'

Al was about to speak again, but Lexi held her hand up. She could hear a noise, and then he could hear it too. It was coming from around the bend in the road and getting louder and closer. It was a horse, moving at a canter on its way to Rouen.

'This could be what we're waiting for,' Al said. 'Whatever it is.'

'Why can't it just be a guy with an envelope that you rip open?' Lexi said. 'Other than that, this is pretty much exactly like *The Amazing Race*, except with people from the past trying to kill you. So, do we hide, or— '

Before Al could answer, the horse had rounded the corner. On its back was a large man with a dark tunic and a gold buckle on his broad leather belt. He slowed down and put his right hand on his sword. He checked the trees to both sides and looked closely at Lexi and Al.

'Move away,' he said. 'You shouldn't be here.' He seemed to be speaking in straightforward English, or at least that was how they heard him.

Al had had all his French ready to go, but it went no further than, *'Bonjour, parlez-vous anglais?'* and he had already been given the answer. Yes, apparently the man spoke *anglais*. But why did he speak it first? Why not French, or whatever Normans spoke in 925? Had they turned up dressed as English people?

'Could you tell us where we are exactly?' Al asked him. 'We got lost in the forest.'

'You shouldn't be here. It's not safe.' The man had a gold badge on his hat, but it had none of the glow of a portal. Behind him, a heavy saddlebag hung over each of his horse's flanks. 'There are outlaws in these woods. They'll rob you, if they haven't already. And worse.' He checked the trees again. His hand was still near his sword. 'You'd be safer in the town. I'm on my way there now, to Lord Rollo's court. He's seeing merchants this afternoon.'

Suddenly, there was a shout. Four men rushed from behind the boulder on the other side of the road. They grabbed the merchant before he could draw his sword, pulled him from his horse and threw him to the ground. One of the outlaws jumped on his scabbard with both feet, and his sword snapped.

Two of them grabbed his arms and started to drag him back across the road towards the boulder. The others cut the saddlebags free of the horse. One of them reached inside, pulled out a coin purse and threw it over to Lexi and Al.

'Don't know who you are,' he said, 'but he wouldn't have slowed down for anyone who looked like us.' He shook the saddlebag and laughed. It was full of money.

The merchant was kicking his legs around and shouting, as one of the outlaws cut at his belt to take the buckle.

From over the hill in the direction of Rouen, a horn sounded. A man on horseback appeared on the road, and then another, then several more – a troop of armed men and,

in the middle of them, a tall man with a beard, long hair and a fur-trimmed cape.

'Ah, Rou!' the merchant shouted, as loudly as he could. 'Ah, Rou! Lord Rollo!'

Several of Lord Rollo's soldiers drew their swords and kicked their horses into a gallop. The outlaws dropped the merchant onto the road and ran, leaving the saddlebags behind. The merchant's leggings had fallen down to his knees and his belt was in pieces.

'Ah, Rou,' Lexi said to Al. 'Ahrou. It's like "Harrow", but without the "H".'

'Where is it? Where's the portal?' Al had the peg ready in his hand.

Lord Rollo's men pulled their horses up, and their hooves sent dust into the air. The outlaws had disappeared among the rocks and trees. There was no sign of a portal yet.

'So, why didn't you two run?' one of the soldiers said to Lexi and Al. 'The rest of your band ran.'

'It was those two who stopped me,' the merchant said. He was getting to his feet, holding the tops of his leggings with both hands. 'They were the bait.'

'No,' Lexi said. 'We were nothing to do with it.' But no one was going to listen to two kids.

Four of the soldiers dismounted and started to move towards Lexi and Al.

'He's got a knife,' the merchant said, pointing to the peg in Al's hand. 'They took money for stopping us. Look.' He pointed to the coin purse, which had fallen at Al's feet.

'He'd better be very clever at using that knife, if he's planning to make a fight of it,' one of the soldiers said as he extended his sword and tapped the peg.

'No, it's not— ' Al took a step back. And then he saw light, golden light, pulsing from inside the coin purse, blinking through the opening, which had come undone when the purse landed.

The soldier grabbed his wrist, gripping it so hard that the peg almost fell. Al tried to pull away, but couldn't. There was a scrabbling sound from Al's bag, and Doug burst free and leapt from Al's shoulder to the soldier's face, scratching and biting.

'Rats!' the merchant shouted. 'They've got a bag full of rats!'

The soldier staggered backwards. His helmet fell off and Doug scrambled into his hair and bit his scalp. The soldier screamed and the other troops fell back.

Al tore the coin purse open and the coins spilt onto the ground. One of them was glowing. All but its rim had been replaced by a golden '& more' button. He touched the button and the portal opened.

Lexi held her arm out for Doug and he jumped from the soldier and scampered along it.

Al threaded the peg through the portal, closed the levers and turned the key.

'Lex,' he said, as the ground started to shake and the mist came in. 'This one didn't say "& more". It said "home".'

As the mist closed in and became a dense fog, they lifted and flew. Days and nights and then years and centuries flickered past, and the world spun like a top – a blur of wars and peaceful lives, cities and empires, wild country and farms and factories, smoke and engines and iron ships, jet planes and satellites.

And a library, with barriers for renovation and a red book on the floor called *Walker & Fuller's Curious Dictionary of English.*

The air smelt of paint and glue. Beyond the barriers someone was talking about a new PlayStation game.

'Lachlan McReadie,' Al said. 'He always wants people to know he got something first.'

Lachlan McReadie's big talk had never sounded better. They were back at school in the 21st century. They were safe.

'I want to hug every shelf in this library,' Lexi said. 'Oh, wow, I actually want to do maths. We've got maths next, haven't we? We made it. We got home.'

Al opened his hand. In his palm he had the fourth peg key. He had two in his bag and one in his sock. He had kept all four. Other than the keys and the whiff of rat vomit in his bag, there was no sign that anything strange had happened.

Doug nudged his way out of the bag and climbed up to Al's shoulder.

'Nice work, buddy,' Al said, as Doug moved to rub himself against Al's neck.

'It was.' Lexi reached over and patted him. 'Good enough to make me touch a rat. He'd better get back in the bag now, though, or you'll get busted.' She took out her phone. 'It's the same time. The exact same time as when we left. You showed me that book right now. You pressed that stupid button right now.'

They both looked at the book.

'We're taking that,' Al said. 'I want to work it out.'

'We're not doing it again. We could have died twice. In the past.'

'I just want to work it out.' He was already picking it up.

They slipped out from behind the barriers and took the book to the counter. Al set it down as if there was nothing special about it.

The librarian, Ms Sharp, went to scan it, but couldn't find a barcode.

'Oh, look,' she said. There was a sticker on the spine. 'That's how they did it a long time ago, that kind of sticker.'

She typed the book's name into her computer. 'It's not in the system. From the look of it, it probably was once, 20 years ago, maybe more. Where did you find it?'

'It was behind something.' Al hoped he wouldn't have to be specific.

But Ms Sharp wasn't really listening. 'Oh, it must have fallen off that pile of old books that we gave to Lifeline a few weeks ago. Are you sure you want to borrow it?'

'Good question,' Lexi said.

'Yes,' Al said. 'This is the one I want.'

'All right.' Ms Sharp took another look at it. 'It's a reference book, though, and usually those have to stay here.'

She opened the front cover. Lexi and Al stepped back without meaning to, in case another glowing button revealed itself.

'No card,' Ms Sharp said. 'They used to have cards, long ago. Why don't you just take it home and bring it back when you're finished with it? It's not in the system at all, so – I'm sure I can trust you to bring it back when you're finished.'

She handed it to Al and he tucked it under his arm, thanked her and headed for the door before she could change her mind. He expected the book to do something strange any second – to glow or buzz or jump free, or expose some weird bit of the past, then and there. But it stayed where he had tucked it, and behaved like a book that was exactly where it needed to be.

'What is it?' Lexi said when they got home that afternoon. 'How do you think it works?'

It was their first chance to talk properly. Their mother was in the study, reading her email, which was usually a mixture of spam, offers of cheap airfares and LOL Cats.

'Don't ask me,' Al said. 'I don't even know if we should open it again. But let's check a few things first. Let's see how much of it really happened.'

'Do you want to get your books?'

Al thought about it. 'I would, but the laptops'll be faster. And less obvious. Imagine if Mum walked out here and you were reading one of Grandad Al's history books.'

He was right. It would be as weird as Al weeding the garden without being asked, or tidying his bedroom. Tidying anything. A year ago he got so sick of their mother saying he'd wake up one night to find rats in his room that he went out and bought Doug.

They both got out their laptops and sat at the table on the back deck. Lexi started with Menlo Park and Al with King William, since he knew some of that story. If their mother came outside or their father got home, it would just look like homework.

'I've found a picture of Edison's lab,' Lexi said after only a couple of minutes. 'It looks like the one we went to. On New Year's Eve 1879, that street we walked down became the first one in the world to get electric lights. And here's "hello".' She swung her laptop around so that Al could see it. 'Here's Thomas Edison wanting to say "hello" when he answered

the phone. It's in a letter from 1877. And Alexander Graham Bell really did want "ahoy". We could be saying "ahoy" now, like a bunch of old sailors. Weird.'

'Instead of saying hello, like a different bunch of old sailors.' Al had found the Wikipedia entry on the death of William II. 'Walter Tyrell was there when William II was killed by an arrow in the New Forest, on the second of August 1100. That's massively creepy, and yet also kind of awesome. I'd never heard of Walter Tyrell before. We couldn't have made that up. We were *there*. Somehow we were actually there, totally in the middle of history, while it was happening.'

'Don't sound so pleased about it.'

Al didn't hear her. He was already clicking on the next link. 'He fled to France.'

'Good call,' Lexi said. 'Walter Tyrell's a – I didn't like Walter Tyrell at all.'

'Lex, look at this.' Al showed her what was on his screen. 'Check the quote. *"Bon archer, bonnes fleches."* That's what the king said the night before. It *is*, "To the good archer, the good arrows," but it's French. Some kind of French. Why didn't Walter Tyrell quote him in French?'

'Maybe he did. Maybe they were all speaking French and somehow we heard them translated.'

'And they understood us?'

'What *is* going on?' Lexi sat back in her chair, away from the laptops.

'Don't ask me.' Al turned his screen back to face him. 'But what a ride.'

Nowhere on the net or in books could Lexi and Al find a site confirming the incident in Normandy as the start of the word 'Hello', though no one could say it wasn't either. No one could confirm anything, and there were theories everywhere.

There were hints of the shout to Rollo here and there in the dozens of possible origins of 'Hello' – references to an old French explanation meaning 'Whoa there', an old English hunting call and, it turned out, to an obscure law still in force in the Channel Islands called 'Clameur de Haro', in which a person being done wrong gives a call for help that begins 'Haro! Haro! Haro!' It was a law that no doubt had its origin in Norman times and, some said, a particular call to Lord Rollo, or Rou, from a man in distress.

'We've seen it, though,' Lexi said. 'Every bit of it. It was a cry for help and then it meant danger or that people should look out. It went from hunting in forests to ships in fog – people on ships calling out to people they couldn't see. And then that idea was borrowed for the phone.'

'I know.' Al had the *Curious Dictionary* on the desk in his room, but he hadn't opened it yet. 'And that's all very interesting, but look at the big picture here, Lex. Something happened with a pretty regular-looking old book and we *travelled through time*. That might be a bigger deal than a bunch of websites that can't tell us where the word "hello" comes from.'

'Travelled through time, or thought we travelled through time, or had some kind of virtual near-death history experience, or got sucked into the pilot of a new reality TV show—' She was still working through a range of options. 'I should have taken photos. *We* should have taken photos. We didn't need a signal to do that.'

As a test, Al had drawn sketches with Lexi out of the room. When she saw them, she confirmed every detail – the lamplighter, the lab, the ship and its rigging, the flushed face of King William and the pinched cheeks of Walter Tyrell.

'I'm still taller than you, though,' she said, pointing to Al's picture of them dressed as 10th century Normans. 'By more than a centimetre. Other than that, what you've drawn is exactly what I saw too.'

Al was pretty sure their height difference was less than a centimetre now, if she was in fact still taller. He'd been catching her all year and would definitely pass her soon. But he wanted someone else to point it out, rather than to demand a measure-off himself.

In the two days since their journey into the past, nothing unusual had happened. Other than the addition of four small peg keys, the world seemed exactly the same as it had been all week. People still said hello and had no clue about why they did it, or that the word might have been more than a thousand years old already, in one form or another.

Al had answered the phone once by saying 'Ahoy' to see what would happen, but Grandma Noela had just replied, 'Well, ahoy, captain,' before getting on with the conversation. Maybe Alexander Graham Bell had been right. Maybe it would have worked just as well.

It was Grandad Al he most wanted to talk to about it, but he had never met Grandad Al.

Alan Hunter had been a teacher at their school until, one day 30 years before, he was nowhere at all. He simply disappeared, without any sign of where he had gone or what had happened.

People who remembered him called him Al, and his grandson, Alastair, eventually became Al, too.

Al and Lexi's father, Mike, was a teenager when his father vanished. Police checked banking records and followed up any sightings, but he was never found.

Alan Hunter had developed a love of history in the years leading up to his disappearance. Afterwards his history books were put in boxes and stayed there, under Grandma Noela's house. Eventually most of his things were parcelled up and put away. Grandma Noela kept hoping that he would turn up, with a good reason for what had happened, and then they could unpack the boxes and get on with life. It didn't happen, but the boxes stayed because she couldn't part with them.

Al was nine when he decided he didn't want his grandfather to be a complete mystery anymore. He asked if he could see the books and he started to read them.

At first he was driven by the idea that Grandad Al's eyes had read those very words, but then history started to fit together in a way that it never had before, like an enormous jigsaw puzzle. One incident, one time, one invention or battle or king led to another and another, and the stories of the past started to connect. Al loved making those connections.

Occasionally, he came upon notes Grandad Al had made on separate sheets of paper and slipped into the books. Mostly he seemed to write when he thought a book had got something wrong, though he didn't say where his new information had come from. Sometimes there were sketches of historical figures or buildings, or a map showing troop movements in some battle.

It was Grandad Al, years after disappearing, who had given Al his enthusiasm for history, and Al wanted to repay him by telling him about 'Hello'.

He didn't know how long he could keep the dictionary, but he wasn't ready for it to go back yet. It was a new connection to the past that his grandad had shown him – even if, as each day went by, Normandy and the New Forest and 19th century America seemed a bit more imagined and a bit less real.

'I want to look inside,' he said, one day when he and Lexi were in his room, with the dictionary on his desk in front of them.

'Only if you use a ruler to open it.' Lexi told herself the book was nothing to be afraid of, but moved to stand behind Al. 'Don't actually touch anything. And be ready to get out of the way. And if anything starts to glow, I'm out of here.'

Al picked up the ruler. He tapped the cover of the *Curious Dictionary* with it, but nothing happened. He touched the edges of the pages. He put the tip of the ruler under the edge of the cover and lifted it open.

On the first page, under the title, was an inscription:

While stories build from words, it's true,
The words themselves have stories too.
Who dares to read? Who dares to look?
Who dares to hunt within this book?

'Okay, shut it,' Lexi said. 'Seeing the word "hunt" is enough for me.'

'What are these?'

Lexi and Al were watching TV with their father when their mother came out of Al's bedroom with his sketches in her hand.

'What were you doing in my room?' Al couldn't think of a good reason to have drawn them.

His mother looked unimpressed. 'If you want to start doing your own laundry, I'm happy to talk about it— '

'Seriously?' Lexi said, looking as though she had never seen the pictures before. 'You've done that much work on the history project already? I've hardly started.'

Their father put down the novel he had just opened and took off his glasses. 'Are they still doing that one?' he said. 'I think they were doing it at Cubberla Creek back when your grandfather was teaching there. He'd always be sketching things like that.'

Al stood up. 'I might put those away, if that's okay,' he said to his mother. 'Don't want them to get out of order.' He needed to check something. He took the sketches and headed for his bedroom, but stopped at the door and turned round. 'And thanks for still doing the laundry, Mum. That's – um – that's fine by me.'

'Good news,' she said. 'Lucky me.'

Al had taken the Ea-Fe volume of Grandad Al's encyclopedia from the shelf by the time Lexi appeared in his doorway.

'You idiot,' she said. 'What are you doing leaving those lying around?'

He didn't look up. He opened the encyclopedia and flipped through the pages. At 'Ed' – with the entry on Thomas Edison – a piece of loose paper slid out and fell to the floor. It was a sketch of the laboratory at Menlo Park.

'I knew it,' he said. 'I knew I'd seen it before.'

Lexi picked it up. 'But why would Grandad Al draw it?'

'Maybe— ' Al had no answer. 'Maybe it really is the kind of thing they did at school 30 years ago?'

Water:
A colourless, odourless, tasteless liquid with molecular composition H_2O

[two atoms of hydrogen and one of oxygen]

[DE waeter].

&
MORE
~

$\mathcal{F}$OR ANOTHER WEEK, the book behaved just like a book. It sat on Al's desk, and then it sat on Al's desk under things – the four peg keys, a book from school, a chip packet. But every time Al walked into his room, it was the first thing that caught his eye, even if he wanted not to look at it. Life wasn't the same now that the *Curious Dictionary* had come along, even if nothing else had changed.

The dictionary held the promise and the threat of another impossible journey. Or maybe it didn't. Maybe, after that one wild ride, it was just a book.

Eventually he and Lexi opened it properly and inside it looked like any other dictionary. They touched the pages and they felt just like pages. No one fell through the floor into another century. Al found an old magnifying glass and they looked at the peg keys closely, but it only made the keys look less special and more like keys from any kind of small lock – one for a suitcase or a mailbox.

Just as they were starting to wonder if they had imagined it all, Al woke up one night in the middle of a dream. There was a glow in the corner of his room, a soft golden light over on his desk. It was coming from between the pages of the *Curious Dictionary*, from somewhere near the end.

He pushed the mess out of the way, but at first he didn't touch the dictionary. Maybe he could hear a humming sound. He couldn't be sure. He put his hand on the front cover. The dictionary was buzzing – faintly, but definitely buzzing.

He lifted it carefully. The desk under it felt warm. He crossed the room with the book in both hands, then held it under one arm so that he could open his door. He picked up his backpack and moved down the dark hallway as quietly as possible. The light from the book was enough for him to find Lexi's doorknob, and he stepped into her room and shut the door behind him.

'Lex,' he whispered. 'Lexi.' She rolled over, but didn't seem to wake. *'Lexi!'*

Lexi sat up. 'What? What are you— ' She put her arm over her eyes. 'I was asleep. Don't come creeping in. Don't frighten me like – Hey, that's not a torch.'

'No.' He held the book out so that it was closer to her. 'Are we going to open it?'

'Why have you got your backpack?'

'The pegs. They've got to go somewhere.' He waited to hear what she would say, but she didn't speak. 'Lex, it's possible – no, it's really likely that we are the only two people in the world who can go back into the past. To see the first electric light, before they'd got it right, to talk to a king from 900 years ago.'

'Yeah, right – and watch him get killed. And then get blamed for it. We don't just get to see history – we get to *be* it.'

Now she could hear the humming. She reached out and put her hand on the book. There was a scuffling, scratching noise as Doug moved around in the backpack.

'We're not taking that rat again,' she said. 'If we go at all.'

'He already saved our lives in the 10th century.'

'Have you opened the book up?' She hadn't decided yet. It seemed crazy even to think about going again – to take the risk – but perhaps the dictionary was a way to the real past, and to things no one else could ever see.

'No,' Al said. 'It looks like the light's coming from somewhere late in the alphabet.'

Lexi nodded. 'Okay.' She got properly out of bed and tried to find shoes. 'Oh, wait a second. We get new clothes each time, don't we? Not that I'm saying I'll go.' She picked up her phone from beside her bed and looked at the book again. 'Okay. Open it.'

Al let the dictionary fall open close to where the light was coming from. The page covered 'umpire' to 'undercoat'. He turned a few more pages, and found 'water' and a bright, buzzing '& more' button. Water sounded safe enough.

'Are we really going to do it?' He looked around Lexi's room, at the 21st century, at a hundred things he needed to take completely for granted to live in his own time. But how many of them would they see where they were going? Maybe this time there would be something to stop them coming back. 'I want to do it. And the last peg brought us home.'

Lexi nodded. She reached out and put her finger on the button.

$\mathcal{T}$ HE FALL WAS a long one, with bumps at the start – small bumps, but at least a century of them, Al guessed. After that they hit smooth air, then a lurch and a less hurried fall, then a bump and turbulence, followed by a sharp drop, a swerve and a clear fall in crisp cool air, and out into the first light of dawn. The cool air felt good after all that.

They were falling over land, but not far from the sea and beaches covered with boats. As the earth came closer, the sea slipped from view and they saw fields with sheep in them, a village that had houses with thatched roofs and, not much further up the road they were about to land on, an army of thousands of men spread out along a hilltop.

They landed with a clanging, clattering sound, like scrap metal falling off a truck. Al looked to see what he had hit. It was a shield in the shape of a long teardrop or a kite, and he hadn't hit it – it was on his arm. He was wearing a tunic of chain mail that made it hard to sit up at first, and to breathe without being really conscious of it. Lexi was wearing one too.

'Oh, that's not fair,' she said. 'I didn't know I'd have to be a soldier if we pressed it. How come that was part of the deal? And what's with this?' She lifted the hat from his head. 'We get little padded leather hats? What's that supposed to do if someone has a go at us with a sword? I'm not doing this without a proper helmet.'

'So you know what we're doing already?' Al wondered if he was missing something.

'As if. I'm just assuming it's not a costume party or a medieval fair.'

She was sitting on something hard, which turned out to be the hilt of a sword. She stood up and drew it from its scabbard, but it was too heavy to hold easily. She let the tip fall to the road, where it scraped in the dirt.

'I can't do a thing with this,' she said, as if it was Al's fault.

She lifted it back into the scabbard with both hands and then became annoyed by a bump under the front of her chain mail. She twisted and pushed at it and squeezed it down far enough that she could reach up and pull it out. It was her phone. She checked for a signal, but there was none. She switched it over to camera mode and pointed it at Al. He made peace signs with both hands and grinned, like all the Japanese tourists he had seen at Surfers Paradise. Lexi took the photo and checked to see that it had worked.

'Got it,' she said. 'It totally looks fake, though. Can I put my phone in your bag? Or should I say sack?'

Al tried to reach the sack over his shoulder, but the chain mail didn't make it easy. 'You'll have to do it. And could you find the peg while you're there?'

Lexi moved behind him, untied the neck of the sack and dropped her phone inside. In the glow from the peg, Doug's two beady eyes looked up at her. His nose was twitching. He could smell sheep and sheep poo, grass, outside toilets.

'There are four this time, I think,' Lexi said, as she took the activated peg out. She turned it over to read it. '1066, and we're near Hastings in England. Is that one you know?'

'Yeah.' This time, Al had no doubt at all, and there was no good way to put it. 'It's the Battle of Hastings. And we're about to be on the losing side.'

'No!' she said. 'No! For *"water"*? "Water" shouldn't take you to a battle. That is so unfair.'

'Because this was all about "fair", wasn't it?' Al was just glad he hadn't pressed the button. He tried to remember the details of the battle, but wasn't sure he'd ever known them. 'We'll hang around the edges, waiting for something to trigger the portal. We'll avoid the worst of it. But I think we have to go to the battle. That's what this gear says. If the battle's where the portal is, we know we can't hide out here waiting for it to come to us.' He sounded calmer than he felt. By now he was getting used to faking it. 'Did you see what it said in the dictionary? "Water" is from Old English. "Waeter". I think this might be the end of Old English. The beginning of the end, anyway, this battle.'

'William II spoke in French. That's 34 years away.' She was thinking it through, too. 'English changed after this. But if we're here in one step, what's next?'

She crouched down, hooked her left arm into her shield and stood up again. She drew her sword and swung it. The effort almost threw her off balance. Al didn't want to say it, but he knew what was next. It didn't matter right now where the pegs might eventually take them, or where 'water' came from. What was next was not being killed at the Battle of Hastings.

'So, we'll stay at the back, then?' she said. 'That's a deal? It's not going to help anyone if we're up the front.'

'Don't worry. No one's going to want us up the front! We stay back, and we look out for the portal.'

No time at all ago – exactly no time, Lexi knew that – she had been safe in her own bedroom, and now here she was, about to walk down a dirt road to join an army and lose a battle.

'The portal couldn't just be in some house nearby, could it?' She was looking around, desperate for any better option to show itself as they walked.

'Well, I suppose it could be anywhere. Some old farmer might jump out and shout something about water and we'd be gone.' As soon as he said it, Al realised that wasn't actually what he wanted. He didn't want to get so close to the Battle of Hastings, and then walk into a field and vanish. 'But think about it, Lex. The Battle of Hastings. This'll be epic. You've got to make sure you've got your phone ready to take photos.'

She stopped dead and turned to face him. 'Are you insane?'

'The Battle of Hastings,' he said, as if she kept missing the point. 'How often do people get to take photos of the Battle of Hastings? One time, and it's us.'

'This way!' It was a voice up ahead. 'Over here.'

Next to some bushes, a man was waving to them. He

was one of a group of soldiers who were wearing padded jackets and carrying axes. Lexi groaned. There was no going back now. No farmer was about to shout 'water' and make it all easy.

'New mail,' the soldier said to Lexi as she and Al approached. He looked about 18 or 20. Thin, but strong. The axe looked like it weighed nothing in his hands. 'Not the full hauberk, but nice nonetheless. Where are you from?'

'Fig Tree Pocket,' she said. She had no idea what a hauberk was, and pretended he hadn't mentioned it.

'I haven't heard of it,' he told her. 'Which county?'

'Kent,' Al said, because one of them had to say something and he knew the Hunters had moved to Australia from Kent in their great-great-grandparents' time. 'What about you?'

'Oh, we're from Guildford. We're the king's men. Not his housecarls, obviously, but we all have land around there, or our families do.' He looked them up and down. 'Doing nicely in Fig Tree Pocket, Kent, then. I'm Wilfred.'

Al stepped forward and then realised he didn't know if people in 1066 shook hands or not. 'I'm Al,' he said. 'And this is – Lex.'

Lexi looked at him. He made sure not to look at her.

'Al and Lex,' Wilfred said. 'Not names I know, but then I suppose I don't know Kent. I've heard a lot of new names this past month travelling up and down the country.'

Wilfred left the other Guildford men and led Lexi and Al to the camp. The more they talked, the more what he said fitted into place. Housecarls were the king's fulltime soldiers and Wilfred pointed out a troop of them as they approached the crest of the hill. They had full hauberks – long shirts of chain mail – laid out on the ground, ready to be put on for battle. The chain mail would reach to their knees and beyond their elbows, in some cases all the way to their hands. With each hauberk was a conical metal helmet, a two-handed battleaxe and a sword.

The equipment carried by the rest of the army was far more varied. These were the fyrdmen, landowners who were part-time soldiers and obliged to equip themselves. Lexi and

Al were fyrdmen, and the king's youngest soldiers looked no older than them.

Wilfred explained that he and the other Guildford men were taking their turn on sentry duty, in case there were Norman raiding parties around. He pointed out the Norman army spread far along the next ridge. There was smoke rising from their fires. And too many soldiers to count or even estimate.

'Let the housecarls take most of it,' Wilfred said quietly. 'That's what they're here for.' He turned to look at the housecarls, as if he needed reassurance himself. Some were sitting nearby in the knee-high grass, eating or playing dice. 'Oh – let me get you something to eat. We've just eaten. Can't see off an invasion on an empty stomach.'

'I want someone to say the word,' Lexi said to Al once it was just the two of them again. 'Whatever we need to hear to get out of this place.'

Wilfred came back with some lumps of hard bread and bowls of a thick soup that didn't taste of much. 'Find some room somewhere and take your armour off for now,' he said. 'You'll get the call when you need to put it on. I'd better be getting back to my post.'

Doug stirred in the sack as soon as the food arrived, but Al didn't let him out until Wilfred was on his way back to the other men from Guildford. Al broke off a small piece of bread and dipped it in the soup, and Doug held it in his front paws and stood up on his back legs to eat it.

'Good call,' Lexi said, watching him. 'I've just tried the bread.'

They found space to sit down at the foot of a tree and, once they had finished eating, Al started unbuckling his sword belt.

'I suppose it's a bit much to hope that they'd have male and female change rooms,' Lexi said, as he set his sword down.

Al laughed. 'It's not Kmart – it's a battle in the 11th century.' He lifted his helmet from his head. 'Lex, I've got two bits of bad news for you. First, there's not only no change rooms, there's also no toilets. Second, these men have no clue you're a girl.'

'How could they not—' It didn't make any sense to her.

'That's why I called you Lex. And I could have done without the glare, by the way. It turns out both our names are ridiculous now anyway. Not only have these men never seen a woman in armour – they can't imagine it. When they look at you, they see my brother. A few hundred years from now, Joan of Arc, when she tries to avoid being recognised before a battle, will do it just by dressing like a boy. And it'll work. These people haven't seen the movies we've seen. They actually look at things differently.'

'That's psycho.' As she moved around to the far side of the tree from the housecarls, she noticed initials carved into the trunk. 'Hey – "TH", "RH", "JH"! The "H"s have been here. We're on track.' She ran her finger along one of the letters, wondering who had carved it there. 'And here's a paperclip.' She picked it up from the ground at the foot of the tree. 'You can't tell me that's 11th century.'

'More like 19th, I think. Maybe even 20th.'

Lexi grinned, for perhaps the first time in 1066.

Within an hour of their arrival, they saw the king. King Harold was in his 40s, and on a tall black horse with chain mail on its chest and flanks. His shield had swirls and circles on it. They looked like ripples caused by stones dropping into water. As he rode through with his guards, the fyrdmen moved aside and bowed.

'We've got to get a photo of this,' Al said, grabbing his sack to look for Lexi's phone. 'I probably can't ask him to smile, can I?'

He hid the spangly pink phone in his hands as well as

he could, and he took a photo of the king from behind, but it was mostly the rump of his horse. A few paces further along, King Harold stopped to speak to some soldiers. He turned and pointed into the distance, at the Normans.

'Got it,' Al said. He showed Lexi the picture, with the king in profile and his troops following his pointing hand.

'Great.' Lexi was already looking beyond the camera.

The housecarls were forming a line along the ridge, fitting themselves next to each other with their shields touching. The Guildford fyrdmen were back from sentry duty and checking that their jackets were properly buckled and their leggings tied.

'Come on,' Wilfred called out. 'If there aren't others here from Fig Tree Pocket, you should join us.'

In the distance, Al could see Norman knights on horses, riding in troops with lances and swords, criss-crossing the lower part of the opposite hill. They were cantering. It was practice for what was to come.

The battle began with the Norman archers moving down the hill. They came much of the way towards the English before stopping and taking up positions. Lexi and Al and the Guildford men fell in behind several rows of housecarls near one end of the English line.

Someone called out, 'Shields up,' and the soldiers around them lifted their shields over their heads. So Lexi and Al did too.

The arrows hit the shields like stones, most of them striking the shield wall of the front rank of housecarls, but a few coming higher and glancing off the shields behind. They heard someone call out in pain not far away, but couldn't see him. They pushed the edges of their shields together.

In the distance, there was shouting from the direction of the Norman lines. They could see nothing from under the shields, but then the order came to lower them. Hundreds of Norman soldiers had passed their archers and were running up the hill with axes and swords.

Al waited for the English archers to shoot at them, but then realised he hadn't seen any soldiers with bows in

Harold's army. From somewhere just behind, a rock flew through the air, then more rocks, javelins and axes. The English were throwing whatever they had. Normans started falling, but those who weren't hit kept coming forward.

'What is that?' Lexi said, pointing to a man nearby who was about to throw something.

Al looked over. 'I think it's a mace.' It was a club with a spiked iron head bigger than a fist.

The man flung it over the housecarls and down the hill. There was no way of telling where it landed.

'We'll be all right,' Wilfred said. 'We'll hold them this time.'

The broken line of Norman infantry crashed into the shields of the housecarls. There was screaming and clattering all along the ridge, orders being shouted into the chaos, men falling and others stepping forward so that the shield wall would hold. Lexi had her sword drawn, but she was resting the tip of it on the ground next to her foot, ready to lift it the moment she had to. All around her, fyrdmen were braced for action. None of them looked as afraid as she felt. They looked wild. They looked ready.

Then it was over. The Normans were falling back.

Next, their cavalry charged and long spears were passed between the English shields to meet them. Again the housecarls held the Normans at bay. A horse fell nearby and knocked three men with shields aside, but the gap in the line was soon filled.

It was Lexi and Al's part of the battle that turned first. As the Normans gave up their charge and retreated, the English fyrdmen, pent up behind the housecarls, pushed through between the shields, picking up fallen axes and maces and throwing them at the enemy. The twins were caught in the surge and carried with the men from Guildford past the fallen bodies and down the hill. The Normans were on the run. There was shouting that the Norman duke was dead, and cheering.

Al wondered if history was changing. He wondered if the English might win. He and Lexi were running next to each other. They had their shields up and their swords ready, but the action was well ahead of them. In only a couple of

minutes, they were nearly at the bottom of the hill and a long way from the housecarls.

Fresh cavalry charged from their right and hit the Guildford men before they knew it. The duke was in the lead – not dead after all.

'His horse was killed,' Wilfred said as he ran up the slope towards them. 'That's all.' There was blood on the sword he was carrying, and on his face. 'Get back. Get back to the shield wall. They'll get us all if we stay out here.'

They heard hooves, dozens of horses, thundering into the men behind them as they ran. Lexi tripped on the uneven ground and fell, but Wilfred stopped to pull her to her feet. She staggered on, dragging her shield, unable to get the breath she needed. Her sword was lost, somewhere back down the hill.

'Go! Go!' Al shouted.

The housecarls' shields opened up to let them through. The charge downhill had been a disaster. Two of King Harold's brothers were dead, along with many fyrdmen. There were more gaps in the shield wall now, and fyrdmen were moving to take up positions where housecarls had been lost.

The Norman archers moved back out onto the battlefield.

Further along the ridge, King Harold raised his sword above his head and began to speak. 'This day will still be ours,' he said. 'This land will still be ours at the end of it. We will not stop until their boats are torched and every last man is driven back to the waeter.'

As soon as the word was said, a symbol at the centre of his shield started to glint with a golden light, though the sun was behind him and the shield in shadow.

'That's it,' Lexi said to Al, just as someone shouted, 'Shields up!'

But there were gaps in the defences now, and the Normans had learnt from the last time their archers had been in action. Now they shot over the shield wall at the men bunched behind.

Lexi and Al had to get to the king. A glow was definitely coming from a point in the middle of his shield.

'Can no one else see it?' Lexi said, as they headed for him. 'Or are they just concentrating on the battle?'

'Look, let's just get there.'

Al focused on the king as fyrdmen pushed past them to fight. The shield wall buckled nearby and the Normans burst through. One hit an Englishman's shield so hard with his mace that the fyrdman overbalanced and fell. Lexi picked his sword up as the Norman jumped on the man's chest with both feet.

As he stumbled from the man's body, he swung his mace above his head and lurched straight at Lexi and Al. Al crouched and lifted his shield. The mace smashed into it and the shield took the blow. Al's arm hurt all the way to the shoulder, and his shield was cracked. The Norman raised the mace again. It would come straight through Al's shield if it hit it a second time. Lexi lunged forward with her sword, and the Norman jumped to avoid it. His mace clipped her

shield instead as it came down, and then it hit her sword arm. It was only a glancing blow, but the studs on the mace tore her skin and she dropped her sword.

As the mace swung away, it was Wilfred who appeared beside her, swinging his own sword into the Norman's chest.

'The king,' Al said. They had to get to the king.

He threw down his useless shield, grabbed Lexi's good arm and pulled her away from the fighting. Wilfred stepped to the left, towards a Norman with an axe.

Further along, the shield wall had not yet broken. Lexi could feel Al pulling her up the hill. She wondered where her shield was. She felt dizzy. She kept bumping into the sack he was carrying. Blood ran from her right hand, down onto the grass. She squeezed her fingers to see if they still worked. Her arm was numb, but her hand moved the way it should.

As they reached the king, another volley of arrows came over the shield wall, hitting a horse, a knight and then the king himself. King Harold's right hand went to his face where the arrow had struck him but his left, with the weight of the shield, fell slack by his side. Another king was dead and Hastings was lost after all.

As Al pulled the king's shield down, Lexi jerked the sack open with her good hand and grabbed the glowing peg. Al touched the portal and it opened. He took the peg from Lexi, jammed it in and locked it. Lexi's knees started to give way. She hooked her arm into Al's belt and turned to look for Wilfred, back in the thick of the fighting. But it was chaos now and he was lost in it somewhere.

As the Norman cavalry smashed the last of the English line, she thought she saw him, or someone like him, still standing, still swinging his sword. Then a mist closed around her and around Al, and the shouts of battle suddenly seemed far away.

*T*HERE WAS A shudder as they entered the portal, then a smooth fall and a lurch sideways. They both felt sick and broke out in a sweat.

Then the sky cleared and the air was fresher and a new land lay below them – a bay with ships and a town.

They landed in a garden, among rows of turnips. There was a two-storey building in front of them and a wall all around made of heaped earth. A man was sitting on a sack of grain, facing them. He was smiling. He was wearing a cream-coloured robe and sandals.

'You need something done to that arm,' he said to Lexi, as if it was the kind of thing he always said to people.

She looked down. Her forearm was throbbing and swollen, and still bleeding. There were no Normans, though. There was no battle. Three more pegs, and the last one would take them home. She was in a robe as well, the same colour as the man's. She couldn't clear the fighting from her head, or Wilfred left in the thick of it, or the mace as it struck her and dug into her skin.

'I have a few things that will help,' the man said.

He lifted a bag onto his lap and beckoned her over. As Lexi stood up, Al jumped to his feet and his hand went to where his sword might be, just in case, but there was nothing on his belt this time.

'You can call me Caractacus,' the man said, 'because it's better than the alternative.' He smiled again, but they had no idea what he meant. 'And your names are— '

For a few seconds, neither of them spoke. They weren't ready for such a normal question, and their names had made no sense in 1066. There were guards on the gate, but Al noticed a woman not far from them sitting weaving a basket. No one was going to attack them, not yet anyway. He knew a peg had activated in the leather bag he was carrying, but he couldn't look at it yet – not with this man talking to them. Lexi was injured and they were lost in the past, but when? And where?

Caractacus took a pouch of leaves and a small bottle from the bag on his lap.

'I'm Lexi and this is my brother, Al,' Lexi said, after Al didn't answer. She was cradling her wounded right arm with her left. The battle was over. She was tired. 'If you could help—'

'Al? You're not Alan, are you?' Caractacus ignored Lexi for a moment.

'No.' It wasn't the kind of question Al had been expecting. 'I'm Alastair.' He wondered how much sense 'Alastair' would make so far back in the past.

'Oh, right. Very good.' Caractacus reached for Lexi's arm and examined her wound closely. 'A mace,' he said in a way that almost sounded like a question. 'I don't think it's broken your arm, though. Had it deflected from something?'

'Yes. A shield.' She didn't know what more to say. The Battle of Hastings was in the future, perhaps centuries in the future.

While Caractacus went to work, Al crouched down and set his bag on the ground. He kept checking all around them – the guards on the wall and the gate, the weaver, a young girl with a dog – but there was no threat, unless it was Caractacus.

Caractacus poured some drops of liquid onto Lexi's wounds and pressed leaves on top.

Al undid the buckle on his bag and lifted the flap. Caractacus seemed to be focusing on Lexi. Doug had the glowing peg in his front paws, and pushed it up so that Al could see it.

The Dark Ages – that was all he knew about 430. It was a big blank, lawless time. In England, anyway. It was after the Romans and before King Alfred and the Venerable Bede. But this was Germania, and he knew almost nothing about Germania.

He dropped the flap down and passed the leather strap back through the buckle. In the dark, Doug twitched his nose at the air that had blown in – turnips, freshly turned soil, farm animals nearby, pigs, chickens, dirty people, armpits – lovely.

Caractacus was winding a strip of cloth around Lexi's arm. The pain was fading even before he had finished.

'It should be going numb now,' he said. He took her other hand and placed it on the end of the bandage. 'Hold that for me, if you could, while I find a pin.' He looked in his bag, then reached into it and dug deeper. 'There's usually one – I try to be ready for anything.'

There was no pin.

'Ah, well,' he said. 'It was there last time. Something special for you, then.'

There was a small casket next to his bag, with gold bands around it and gold corners. There were pictures on each of its sides made of jewels set in gold and silver. One side had a chariot with a king on it, and one end had stones arranged to look like a shell in a blue sea. He picked up the casket – which was heavier than it looked – and opened it. It was full of jewels and gold. Belt buckles, headpieces and pendants. He found a brooch with a pin on the back.

'Say nothing about this,' he told them as he lifted Lexi's hand away and fastened the bandage with the brooch. 'Not ever, but particularly not today in this king's court.' He straightened the edges of the bandage and then turned to Al. 'And you know to say nothing about *any* of this, don't you? Not to anyone.'

Al wasn't sure how to answer. It had been more of an instruction than a question. Lexi still looked dazed. Caractacus seemed to know something. He looked right through them in a way no one else had been able to. For a moment, Al thought he could even mention Hastings and Caractacus would know about it. He did a quick calculation: 636 years. That was how far in the future it was. Caractacus couldn't know. Caractacus couldn't know anything about what they'd been doing.

But Caractacus had already moved on. He was closing the casket and putting it on the ground between his feet. The brooch had a green stone that caught the sunlight and had gold spun around it, in some places not much thicker than a hair. Lexi stared at it. Some of it looked like writing.

'"Vortigern ordered me made."' Caractacus had noticed her trying to read it. 'That's what it says. In one of the languages of the Britons. You won't even recognise all the letters. That bandage will do until you get home, but when you do, make sure you have the wound checked again.' He looked around, to make sure there was no one close by. 'Let me tell you why I'm here.'

He explained, as if it was important for them to know, that the treasure casket was a gift from the Britons to King Offa of the Angles. Caractacus was an ambassador for

Vortigern, the High Lord of the British Senate, and he had come to Angeln to negotiate peace.

'But there will be no peace,' he said. 'Vortigern brought the Angles to Britain – and the Saxons – to be our soldiers and defend our towns against the Picts and the Scots. He brought enough to make an army, and they decided to become one. They rose against him and have taken lands they are already calling Sussex and Essex – the lands of the south and east Saxons. Vortigern calls himself king now, and each year he's king of less and less. I'm here to plead for peace with King Offa, and to negotiate the price of it. But have you seen the ships in the bay? They're not built for fishing. My ship's among them, with the crew ready, but the rest are King Offa's warships.'

It was supposed to make more sense to Lexi and Al than it did. The only King Offa Al had heard of wasn't born yet and Lexi wasn't really listening. Her mouth was dry and she was starting to feel dizzy again. Perhaps it was because of the medicine Caractacus had used to treat her arm, or maybe this was just how you felt after surviving a battle – after the shock of it happening all around you, the men screaming, the thousands of brutal fights between men that added up to make history, one way or the other. She realised she didn't know what year it was now, or where they were.

A man was standing at the corner of the building. How long had he been there? Al looked wary, ready.

'Lord Ambassador,' the man said to Caractacus, 'the king will see your party now.'

Al realised he was referring to the three of them. He and Lexi were dressed in robes so that they could go with Caractacus.

Caractacus picked up the treasure casket and stood.

'I'll bring your bag,' Al said, lifting it from the ground.

'Very good,' Caractacus said. 'And, um – ' He tried to remember Lexi's name. 'Your injured arm. Fold a little of your robe over the bandage, but make sure they can see both your hands.'

They were led around the building to an outside staircase that took them up to the second storey. There were two guards on the door, each wearing leather armour and carrying a spear.

King Offa was inside, at the far end of the room, sitting on bear skins draped over a wooden throne. He had a gold goblet in one hand and was looking out a window. On the floor below a pig squealed and animals could be heard digging around in straw. The king's chamber smelt like a barn, and downstairs it seemed that there was one.

'Lord King,' Caractacus said, as he gave a short bow. 'We come in the name of Vortigern, High Lord and King of the Britons.'

Offa shifted around on the throne to make himself more comfortable. He rearranged his cloak. A servant reached forward to help straighten it and Offa acted as if the man wasn't there.

'We bring gifts of friendship,' Caractacus said.

He held the casket out and, keeping their heads bowed,

two men took it to the king. They placed it in his hands and backed away silently. King Offa opened the clasp, lifted the lid and looked inside.

'You can't have many friends,' he said, 'if this is how you treat them. Or do the Britons make friendships that can fit in tiny boxes?' He smiled and his guards all laughed until he raised his hand for silence.

'My Lord, we seek a lasting peace,' Caractacus said. 'On terms favourable to both kings.'

King Offa closed the casket. One of his guards stepped forward to take it from him and place it on a nearby table.

'There will be peace,' King Offa said. 'And I will be happy with the terms. I will bring my armies to Britain, I will be your king and there will be peace. We have built a fleet and you have seen it. Count our ships before you leave and assume more than a hundred men in each. Tell our people in Britain to prepare to welcome us to our new Angle land. We are set to cross the wettir.'

In the dim light of the chamber, the glow from one end of the casket was instant and bright. Al noticed that Caractacus had seen it, but none of the others seemed to.

Al slid the bag from his shoulder and reached inside.

'We have another gift, Your Majesty,' he said, as he drew the golden peg from the bag. 'It fits with the first, if I may—'

He started to step forward, his head bowed a little, and Lexi followed.

'I can't say it'll be persuasive,' Offa said, raising one eyebrow.

The stone in the middle of the shell design on the end of the casket was now a glowing '& more' button. Al touched it and the portal opened up. He put his hand on the lid, drove the peg in and locked it down. As he turned the key, the room shook and mist rolled in through the windows. Only Caractacus appeared steady, and he was moving towards the door.

L EXI AND AL fell through pale mist and thin air, dropping quickly and straight down.

The mist parted and they were in sunshine, above a forest that went as far as they could see. On the bank of a river, on the largest patch of grass and directly below them were tents in rows.

They landed between a pile of empty clay jars and a boar that had been hung from a hook by its trotters. Doug scrambled to the top of Al's bag, but couldn't push his way out. He poked his nose through and sniffed hard – trees, damp leather, sweaty feet and, yes, an enormous cooked pig. The thought of it made him lightheaded, and he flopped back into the bag. How much pig could he fit in there without anyone noticing?

Lexi felt much better. Her head was clear. She checked her arm. She moved her fingers and her wrist and the pain was gone, for now at least. She looked closely at the brooch, still trying to work out how the letters said what Caractacus had told her.

Al was already taking the activated peg from his bag. 'Let me see it too,' she said. 'You're not the only one here.' At first she thought there was something wrong with the peg. It couldn't be a year with only one digit. Could it? 'Like 2,000 years. Have we really gone back 2,000 years?'

Al was looking around at the tents. 'Whoa. This has to be the Roman army.' Someone beyond the tents was giving orders.

'People really didn't know how to make pants in the past, did they?' Lexi was ignoring what he said for the moment.

Al was wearing a cloak fixed by a clasp over a tunic and off-white leggings, and his bag was a leather satchel hung by two bronze rings from a pole. It looked as if he had to carry it over his shoulder. He crossed his legs and smoothed down his tunic, but that didn't help.

'We look like we're safe, though. We look like people from a Roman camp, like we're supposed to be here. We're not the enemy.' He patted his cloak to see if he had any weapons. No – worse luck. 'Wonder which legion it is?' he said. 'It might be Julius Caesar! No, too late.'

'Before you start thinking about your autograph book again, there are the "H"s, or at least a couple of them.' She was pointing at an empty jar with 'TH' scratched onto it. Next to it, 'RH' was written in what looked like sauce, as if it had happened only minutes before.

Al wondered if they were nearby – RH, TH, maybe others.

'I hope it's not another battle.' Hastings kept coming back into Lexi's head. So did Wilfred. She took a deep breath. She could hear the river rushing over stones. 'The year 9.' In the distance, she could see soldiers upstream, fishing. 'I should take some photos while we've got the chance.'

She reached for Al's bag and found her phone, but her Hastings photos were gone. The last picture was from real life, her friend Amelia with a cup of bubble tea, crossing her eyes and sucking tapioca balls up a fat straw.

'Not happy,' she said. 'I can't believe I went through all that and I don't even have one shot.' She stared at the picture of Amelia. Real life looked easy, in a way it never had before. Easy, predictable, safe. 'And before you say anything, I didn't delete them by mistake. They were definitely there. I was okay when I took them.' She rested her injured arm in her lap.

'Hey, you've still got that fat jewel.' Al pointed to her bandage. 'That's not bad.' He wanted the Hastings photos to be there more than Lexi did, but they weren't, and there was no point arguing about the reasons. He needed her to stay positive. 'And 430 was better than 1066, even if the king did seem to be living with pigs. What was up with that Caractacus guy, though?'

'Yeah,' she said. 'He was different. He didn't even seem surprised that we were suddenly there, sitting on the veges, me with my arm mashed by a mace. It was like he was ready with the first-aid kit.'

'I'm sure he knew something. Or maybe it was just a look that he had. I don't know. I think he could see the portal. I didn't know if anyone other than us could.'

'Why? You think you're like the Chosen One from those movies? The freak with the special power?' Lexi could remember Al at five putting on a cape and jumping off things until he broke his arm.

'Not everything is an opportunity for you to call me a

freak.' It was a relief to Al that she was back to paying out on him. She seemed less dazed, finally.

'Maybe not *everything*.' She picked up her phone again. 'Anyway, there was that guy on the other boat off Nantucket – the one who shouted out. I thought he might have seen it.'

'He might have just thought the boats were going to hit.'

Lexi started lining Al up. He moved into a kneeling position to hide his legs, and straightened his tunic out again.

'Yeah, do that,' she said. 'You look like a girl in the front row of a class photo.'

'Cheruscans!' a voice called out from the tent in front of them. 'Cheruscans, where are you?' The tent flap was pushed aside and a man stepped out. He had a big belly and food stains down his front. 'Your lord has sent for food,' he said to them. 'I'm not going to give it to a Roman to carry to him. Come in here, both of you.'

They followed him into the tent. There were bowls of fruit and plates of meat on two trays. Doug started scrabbling around in Al's bag. Al shook it and he stopped.

'He's with the governor now.' The cook pointed across the clearing, in the direction of a tent with about ten Roman guards outside it.

Al took the heavier tray, though it was difficult to carry with his bag on a pole. He watched Lexi as she lifted hers. 'I'm okay,' she said. 'My arm feels pretty normal now.'

As they crossed the grass, Al scanned the camp trying to get an idea of the number of soldiers there, and how well armed they were.

'So, we're not Romans,' Lexi said.

'No, we're Cheruscans.' He could tell that she was waiting for more. 'Don't ask me who the Cheruscans are. But our boss is with the governor. And we haven't got any weapons.'

'Okay, don't even start about weapons.'

One of the guards ahead of them opened the tent flap. 'Tell General Varus the food is here,' he said quietly to someone inside.

Lexi and Al stopped in front of the tent. What were they supposed to say next? They decided to keep their mouths shut and wait for an order.

Someone inside spoke to the guard and he drew the flap all the way back this time and nodded for them to go in.

'Ah, good,' a man said. He was dressed in the same style as them, though the clasp that fastened his cloak was gold. He had blue eyes and fair hair. 'Over here, please.'

He cleared space on a table and the Romans with him looked on. They were senior soldiers, all older than him. It was clear which one was the general. He was standing at the head of the table.

'So, we'll enter your father's lands today, Arminius,' he said to the Cheruscan, ignoring the food for now. 'And you'll do it as a Roman of high rank.' He sounded as if he was testing him.

'I've learnt from Rome,' Arminius said. 'Even if I did it as a hostage at first. The rest of my tribe can learn too. It's better to be in the tent.'

'And you would go north, rather than northeast?' The general pointed to the map that was open in front of him.

'The path is narrow, but north takes us into the heart of Cheruscan land,' Arminius told him. 'We can travel freely there. Our enemies – Rome's enemies – are to the east of the Cheruscans, but they are expecting a direct attack from where we are now. We'll destroy them in one assault if we attack them from another direction.'

Lexi and Al had read maps for camping and bushwalking, but the Roman map made no sense to them, and not because it was upside down. It was long and narrow, with zigzag lines and pictures of houses and larger buildings that presumably meant cities and towns. At the top and one side, the lines and buildings ran out. The general had pointed there, to spaces that were blank except for a blue line or two that might be rivers.

'We'll eat,' he said and looked along the table to the two trays of food. 'Then we'll march.' He turned to the other officers. 'The 17th Legion, followed by the 18th and the 19th. The Cheruscans are to go with the 19th. You're with me at the head of the 17th, Arminius. You're happy to be separated from your men?' Although it sounded like a question, it clearly wasn't to be answered. 'Bring a few with you so we don't scare the natives. Bring these two.' He glanced towards Lexi and Al. 'They're small. They're not likely to scare anyone.'

As the armies crossed the river and marched off the map, Lexi and Al were at the front, with the general and Lord Arminius and their personal guards.

'I'm pretty sure we're the only people here not likely to scare anyone,' Lexi said quietly to Al.

At first they could all march four abreast along the path, but it soon narrowed. After an hour, they were down to two abreast, and then one. The path rose among the hills and was often steep. The ground turned wet and boggy and the march became a trudge. The white legs of the general's horse were spattered with mud.

'There can be storms in these hills,' Arminius explained to him when he started complaining. 'Even when the sky is clear where we camped.'

The Legate of the 17th Legion was in front of both of them, and he turned in his saddle. 'We're vulnerable, General,' he said. 'We'd have no chance of going into battle formation here.' He scanned the trees above and below the path.

'There should be no need for that,' Arminius said. 'There might be a few outlaws in the forest, but you can't tell me three legions of the Roman army make a tempting outlaw target.'

The general laughed. 'Stop worrying, Marcus. The battle won't be today, and it won't be here.'

At times the mud was halfway up to Lexi and Al's knees, and squishing in their sandals. As the path dipped ahead of them and rose again, they could see a river below them through the trees. On a bushwalk, they would have had three or four breaks by now.

As the leaders started up the rise to the next bend, Arminius stopped his horse. The other Cheruscans stopped too.

He pulled a horn from his cloak and blew it, three long blasts. The Cheruscans drew their swords and formed a circle.

A row of men appeared on the ridgeline above, with another behind them. They were running already, charging down the hill and through the trees with axes in their hands.

Somewhere up there, another horn blew, then another, carrying the signal back to the assembled army.

'It's a trap!' the Legate shouted at his troops. 'Kill the Cheruscans! Form battle lines!'

The soldiers of the 17th Legion turned on Arminius and his men, and Lexi and Al were in battle once again. Al slipped in the mud and dropped his bag as a Roman charged at them, and both he and the Roman overbalanced and fell. Al dived for the handle of the Roman's fallen sword as the man grabbed his legs. Lexi picked up the soldier's shield and brought it down on his head with all the strength she had.

Al was still on his knees when the next soldier came at him. He swung the sword and the Roman swerved out of the way, but then came forward again. He used his shield to block Al's next strike, just as Lexi moved to shove him with the shield she was holding. The Roman's feet slipped out from under him and he fell into the mud. A Cheruscan swung his axe at the Roman's chest. Lexi looked away as it hit with a crunch.

Most of the Roman soldiers had moved uphill from the path to meet the charging Cheruscans on firmer ground, but General Varus's guard and some of the 17th had stayed back and were moving to encircle Arminius and his men. The Cheruscans were holding them, but they were outnumbered five to one.

Lexi felt a hand on her shoulder and turned, ready to strike again with her shield. It was Arminius.

'Go,' he said. 'You haven't seen enough battle for this. You two go to the wattar.' He was pointing down the hill, towards the river. 'You'll be safe there. Your time for this will come.'

'Wattar!' Lexi shouted to Al. 'We've got it.' She was looking for the glow of the portal, but couldn't see it.

Al was battling a Roman, each of them beating the other's shield with his sword. Lexi pushed forward and brought her shield next to Al's. They pushed the Roman hard and he staggered backwards.

'Run!' she screamed, grabbing Al's arm.

He dropped his shield and picked his bag up from the ground as she pulled him away. The last gap in the Roman ranks closed behind them as they escaped. Al shook his bag free of the wooden pole and tucked it under his left arm. He still had the sword in his right hand.

'Where's the portal?' he shouted. 'What if it's back there?'

'I didn't see it.' Lexi knew it was possible that they were running away from it. 'But we couldn't stay. We had a while to get to King Harold. It's not like it's just there for a few seconds.'

She checked over her shoulder. They were clear. The fight was back in the trees and she could see no Romans coming after them. There was no glow of any portal either, and she would definitely be able to see it in the deep shade of the forest. They were most of the way to the river now.

Doug shrieked from the flap of Al's bag, and Al whipped round just in time to see two men in grey robes lunging at him from the bushes. He lifted his sword as one of them tried to bring a tree branch down on his head, and the branch snapped on the blade.

The second man kept low, diving for Al's legs, and it was instinct that made Al bring the sword down. The point of it struck the man's back and Al felt something snap and give way. The man's hands grabbed at the fallen leaves, he groaned and then lay still.

'I can see the portal,' Lexi said. 'It's in the water.'

The other man in grey ran off and Lexi grabbed Al's arm. In shallow water close to the riverbank, a stone was glowing.

'The peg!' she shouted at him, but he didn't seem to hear.

Al was fixed to the spot where he stood, pale and staring at the man he had stabbed.

'Get the peg out!' She pulled him around and reached into his bag.

All Al could think about was the feel of the sword as it struck the man, as it found resistance, and pushed through it.

Lexi went down on her knees on the riverbank and reached into the water. She touched the stone and drove the peg into the hole as it opened up. She brought the levers down and turned the key.

$\mathcal{T}$HERE WERE BUMPS at first, then a lurch sideways and a long, long fall, ending with a massive crunch as the air cleared. They were above grasslands, rocky hills and a river. There were mountains in the distance.

Directly below, a city took shape. They could make out its walls, which were built from the stone of the hillside, and clusters of buildings, and a square. There was smoke spewing from it. The city was burning. There were people in the square, hundreds of them.

The largest building, perhaps a palace or castle, stood inside an inner wall. Al thought they might land on the wall, but they skidded down the outside of it and landed on some stairs that led below ground.

'I think I might have killed that guy,' Al said. He couldn't get the sensation out of his mind. His arm could still feel it, as if it had a memory too.

'You don't know that.' They were in an ancient burning city and she needed him to focus. 'He might have got help.'

'Lex, I stuck a sword in his back.' It was a horrible thought. 'And it was the year 9, in a forest. Who was going to help?'

'He was going to kill you. You had no choice. Get a grip! Where are we? Where's the peg?'

141

Al didn't move, so she found the final peg in his sack. There was shouting not far away, dozens of voices. Was it from people putting out the fire, or was the city being attacked?

'We're massively BC now,' she said, showing him the peg. 'What's Hattusa? Who are the Hittites and what happens here?'

Al had no answers. Lexi had never seen clothes anything like the ones they were wearing. Maybe pictures of ancient Egyptians came close.

'We get through this and then we're home,' she said to him. 'Let's find somewhere safe and try to work out what's happening.' There was no way to climb the walls, and running out of the alley they had landed in seemed like too big a risk. 'The stairs. We must have landed here for a reason, and maybe it's them.'

She led the way down, not knowing what they might find. The passage was dark at first, but, at the end of it, flickering orange light spilt through a doorway.

'Quickly! Quickly!' a man's voice said from inside the room. 'I can't do all this on my own and the Kaskians will be here any minute.'

Lexi and Al stepped through the doorway. The man was small, with dark hair and olive skin. His hat was taller than his head.

'Who are you?' He glowered at them. 'I said I needed two strong men.'

'I'm Lexi and this is Al,' Lexi said.

'What kind of names are those? They're not Hittite. Where are you from?' He looked closely at what they were wearing. 'But you belong to the court, King Suppi's court.'

'King Soupy?' Lexi tried hard not to laugh.

'Suppiluliuma II. Don't tell me you don't call him Suppi behind his back.'

'Of course. And you are—'

Now he managed to look confused and annoyed at the same time. 'Mursili. Court librarian. The man you've been sent to help.'

There was a crashing noise outside.

'Move,' Mursili said. 'First we block the entrance.'

He went to the doorway, wound a handle and a sheet of stone slid slowly down into place. Together they lifted the other stones that would lock the door into position, and pushed them into the grooves that had been cut for them. It took all three of them to lift the largest one.

'Right. Now to move the documents to the vaults in the inner palace.' Mursili looked around. There were rows and rows and piles of clay tablets with neat pointed writing pressed into them.

'Is this Egypt?' Al thought he had seen that kind of writing before.

'I'm going to pretend you didn't say that,' Mursili said, 'because it's so peculiar, and so rude. And because the Kaskians are attacking. Take those first.' He pointed to a pile of tablets tied together with rope. 'You want to know about Egypt? Later you should read those. That's the peace treaty we struck with them after we beat Ramses II at Ashkalon. We drove Egypt to its knees that day. Look at what they had to pay us.'

There was a commotion on the steps outside and something pounded into the stone door. After a few seconds, it pounded again, but the door didn't budge.

'Take them,' Mursili said. 'Take everything you can through the passage—' He pointed somewhere over his shoulder, off in the dark. 'Pile it in the second-last vault and then come back. I'll stay here sorting out what's next. We'll take the most important ones and then we'll seal the passage.'

Al picked up the tablets and Mursili filled Lexi's arms with more. There was smoke in the chamber now, seeping in from somewhere.

'Quickly!' Mursili said, and they started to run.

They threw long shadows as they ran away from the light. They passed rows of tablets filed against each other like books. There was a distant rumbling ahead of them now – and more smoke. But they kept going.

Something just beyond and above them made a cracking sound. With a boom and a rush of dust and smoke, the passage to the inner palace collapsed.

'Back to Mursili!' Al shouted. 'Maybe there's another way.'

Mursili watched them hurrying towards him. He knew what had happened. And he knew there was no other way.

'Put the tablets down,' he said.

Through the stones of the fallen passage walls, they could see flames. The inner palace had been breached and was burning. Smoke billowed into the chamber.

'I can't—' Mursili was trying to think of an answer.

'Water,' Lexi said. 'Is there something here about water?'

'There's nothing here that would stop that fire.'

'On the tablets. Anything written about water? Just show me. Don't ask me to explain.'

'Wattar— ' He waved his hand at the smoke, then lifted his robe to his face. 'There are 30,000 tablets.' He coughed.

'He's triggered it,' Lexi said to Al. 'It's somewhere here. Wattar.' She was already looking round for the glow.

She went over to Mursili and tugged at his robe until he lowered it from his face.

'Wattar,' she said to him. 'Where would it be written? Where's the most likely place?' He looked at her blankly. 'Please! I need you to be a librarian now.'

That seemed to trigger something.

'Ignore taxes and treaties,' he said. He pointed to where they were. 'You check ceremonial procedures,' he said to

Lexi, indicating which rows. Then he turned to Al. 'You check palace domestic records. They're just behind you. I'll do laws. I know which bits to look at. We have water laws.'

He started tipping tablets over on a nearby shelf, looking for the symbols for wattar. Al and Lexi did the same, but faster.

'Don't worry about reading everything,' Al shouted out to him. 'It'll glow when you see it. Or it might not. It'll glow for us at least. We'll see it.'

'What?' Mursili was on his knees now, trying to keep below the worst of the smoke. 'That makes no sense at all.'

The torches in the chamber were going out as the smoke smothered them and the room was growing darker. The smoke caught in Al's throat as he saw it – a faint golden light from between two tablets further along the row. He ran there and pulled them out. Two characters burnt brightly.

'I've got it!' he shouted. 'Lex, this way.'

Lexi crouched down and ran.

'What? What's going on?' Mursili yelled as he stumbled across to them. 'How will that tablet save us?'

'Al,' Lexi said. 'We have to take him with us. He'll die if he stays here.'

'Can we?' Al had taken the peg from the bag. 'Could it wreck the whole thing?'

'Who knows? But we have to try.'

Al touched the characters and they changed shape, forming the word 'home'. The 'O' widened and glowed fiercely. Al drove the peg through it, pulled the levers and turned the key.

'What strange magic is this?' Mursili said, stepping back at exactly the wrong time. 'A rod that passes into a tablet— '

As the smoke thickened and they lifted away, Lexi saw Mursili's arm reaching for them, and then everything went dark.

They flew on and on, for 3,000 years and for exactly no time at all. The smoke cleared and the air grew impossibly thin. Then a gust of wind blew in, smelling of gum trees and night and Fig Tree Pocket.

They were in Lexi's room, with the dictionary on the floor.

'The past is *insane*,' Lexi said, as soon as she had steadied herself. 'I am so not going back there.'

'I think I killed a Roman,' Al said. 'Or someone. A monk. We just about got killed all over the place. And the word water didn't really change for 3,000 years.'

'Yes.' It was sinking in for Lexi too. 'Way back in the BC time, little guys with crazy hats living in places you have

149

never heard of said "wattar" when they meant water. It's practically identical.'

'I wonder where he is,' Al said. He looked around Lexi's room. It was exactly the same as it had been a minute before, when they had opened the dictionary. Mursili wasn't with them. 'I hope he got out of there.'

Doug climbed out of Al's backpack and up onto his shoulder. He took his first big sniff of home smells. The stink of the past was excellent – meat, poo everywhere, dirty people – but it was good to be back, even if the 21st century was a bit too clean.

'Hey, wait – that guy in Germania couldn't have been a monk.' Al tried to picture the man's face, or any detail other than his robes. 'It was 9AD. There were no monks then. What was he? Was he even real? Was any of it?'

Lexi turned her bedside light on. There was a dull throbbing pain in her arm. Maybe it had been there in Germania and Hattusa, but it hadn't been safe to feel it until now.

'Some things are real. The bandage is real, and it looks like I get to keep this.' She turned her arm so that Al could see Vortigern's brooch.

'I can't believe that made it all the way home,' he said. 'It's a 1,500-year-old brooch made by a king and you get to keep it and you don't even notice history!' He stopped himself. He had been okay with it when the brooch had made it to 9AD, but it was harder to cope with the idea of an amazing relic of the past being tossed into one of Lexi's drawers with junk bought from markets and home-made Ron Weasley badges. He had to remind himself of what Lexi had gone through. 'Okay, you did get whacked by a mace.' He reached out and touched the brooch. 'I wonder how it got to come back with us, when we do a total costume change every time we go through a portal.'

'I don't know.' She moved to hold her right arm in her left. It hurt less that way. 'Maybe it's something to do with that Caractacus guy.'

'Next problem: how do we explain the bandage? People are going to notice. And it's not as though you can just take it off. It's there for a reason.'

'We tell Mum and Dad it's from the bushwalking first-aid kit. I tripped in the dark. I was going to the bathroom.' She stood up and headed for the door. From the top of the bookcase she picked up a glass bowl. It had an old phone recharger in it and some paperclips. She tipped them out. 'I knocked this over when I was falling and I landed on it. Could you hold my art folio underneath?'

She wrapped a thick sock around her hand and, while Al held the art folio in place, she broke the bowl against the corner of the bookcase. She let the pieces fall onto the art folio.

'I never liked that bowl anyway,' she said, as she checked the sock for glass. 'Could you get a bag that we can put all that in? And take a bandage out of the bushwalking first-aid kit?'

The next morning, their mother was too concerned about Lexi's injury to notice the brooch. Not that she kept track of Lexi's brooches anyway – there were too many of them for that.

The clinic opened at eight on Sundays, and they got there five minutes before.

'I don't understand how you could get hurt without me knowing,' she said, as they waited for the doors to be opened. She swapped her sunglasses for her regular glasses and peered through the doors into the darkened waiting room. 'I don't know how I didn't wake up. You should have told me.'

'I told you this morning.' Lexi tried to sound confident. If she really had hurt herself in her room, she would have shouted for her parents. 'Al and I fixed it. We did that first-aid course.'

The lights went on inside and the receptionist came over to unlock the doors. She took one look at Lexi's bandage and said, 'You'd better go straight through to the treatment room.'

'You can stay in the waiting room,' Lexi said to her mother. 'I know this stuff makes you feel sick. That's why it's good you're an accountant.'

'I'm not sure I'm ready for you to be this independent.' Her mother took a half-step, as if she might come anyway.

'Don't be embarrassing. You'll have paperwork to do. Then they have magazines.' She pointed to a pile of magazines on a table. 'I'll be okay.'

She would be okay. She knew it. Having a wound fixed was nothing compared to being mashed by a mace at the Battle of Hastings, or smashing a Roman soldier with a shield. She didn't want her mother to see the leaves or exactly what the wound looked like, but she realised she also didn't need her there. She wouldn't have gone into the treatment room a week ago without one of her parents.

'That's nice,' the nurse said as she unclipped the brooch and slid the pin from the bandage.

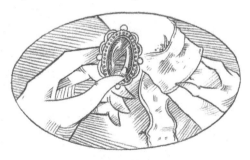

'It's almost a hundred years old,' Lexi told her. 'It was the first thing we found with a pin.'

The nurse clipped the pin back in place and Lexi put the brooch in her pocket.

'How old's your first-aid kit?' the nurse said, as she unwound the bandage from Lexi's arm. She was rolling it up as she went. 'Bandages are usually stretchier.'

The doctor came into the treatment room before Lexi had a chance to answer. The leaves were starting to show.

'What have you got in there?' he asked her. He was a doctor she hadn't seen before. He had a stethoscope around his neck and small round glasses.

'It's bush medicine,' she told him. 'We learned it in first aid. We've got the tree at home.'

'Really?' He pulled up a stool and looked at the wound more closely. He picked up forceps from a tray and peeled a leaf away. 'What is this? I don't recognise it. On the other hand, I don't know much about trees, I suppose. And we have dressings made from components of seaweed, so— '

He lifted all the leaves off, one at a time. Lexi's arm was swollen and the studs on the mace had torn her skin away.

'It must have been quite a fall,' the doctor said. He bent his arm around and tried to imagine the position she'd been in.

'I was sleepwalking,' she said. 'I might have even been standing on the bed.'

Lexi's arm felt sore and stiff all day.

After dinner that night, their father said, 'Lexi's turn to pick what we watch on TV. She's had a rough time.' He opened the TV guide. 'There's football. Two kinds of football. ABC1's got a documentary on the Battle of Hastings—'

'I *hated* the Battle of Hastings.' It was out before she could stop herself.

Her father was giving her a strange look. 'No pressure. Plenty of other choices.'

'At school,' she said. 'I hated it at school. It was so boring.'

'I'm amazed how much history they still teach at that school. And people say the basics have gone out of education.' He looked back at the TV guide to see what else was on. 'But you're right. It can be boring. When it's just dates and numbers, it's not interesting. You should have heard your grandfather talk about the Battle of Hastings. "If only the English had had archers." You need something to make it come to life. He could do that. "If only the English hadn't broken their line, they wouldn't have all been wiped out."'

'Wiped out?' The thought made Lexi feel sick. Al knew it was Wilfred she was thinking about.

'Pretty much.' Their father had picked up the remote, and he was pointing it at the TV. 'But don't quote me. His stories were great, but they did go on a bit.'

In an ad break, Al left the room. He googled the battle and found out what he could. He came back in to the sound of a sitcom laugh track. Lexi was staring at the TV screen, but he could tell that she was paying no attention to it.

'Might go and load the dishwasher,' their father said. 'Watch whatever you want.' He slid the remote across the coffee table in Lexi's direction.

'Where's Mum?' Al said as soon as he was gone.

'Emails.' She lifted her injured arm from the cushion in her lap and set it down gently on the arm of the chair. 'Wiped out. Did you hear that?'

'That's what I've been checking. The housecarls were wiped out. Some fyrdmen got away. Let's hope he was one of those.'

'Let's hope. He was right in the middle of it. We should have taken him.'

'We can't just *take* people.' Changing history seemed wrong, but he knew they'd already done it, or at least tried to with Mursili. 'I don't know what we can do. I hope he was okay. I googled Caractacus too. There's no Caractacus in the 5th century that I can find. There was a British King Caractacus who fought the Romans a few hundred years earlier. And an Angle king called Offa in the 5th century. And pretty much everyone who's ever thought about England in 430 is happy to dump on Vortigern. But the Caractacus we met is a bit of a mystery, or just not a big enough deal to be remembered.'

'The photos on my phone are gone,' she said quietly. 'I meant to tell you. The ones from the Roman camp as well, which I definitely, definitely saved. Every picture I took. I just don't get it – and I'm really not sure I want to.'

Lexi persuaded Al that the *Curious Dictionary* was too dangerous to keep. Too much of the past seemed to be about killing or being killed. It had to go back to the library. Al squeezed it into his backpack the next morning and they took it there before school started.

Ms Sharp was at the counter again.

'Oh, yes, this one,' she said, when Al handed her the dictionary. 'You got everything you needed from it?' She went to put it down on the counter, but stopped. 'Oh, hang on a second. This is the one Mr Bogazkale wanted to talk to you about.'

'Right,' Al said. He had never heard of Mr Bogazkale.

'He's in his office.' She pointed to one of the librarians' offices behind her. 'He wanted to check something with you. You should probably take the book too.'

Lexi and Al went over to the door and knocked on it.

Inside the office, a drawer in a filing cabinet slid shut. Someone coughed and then said, 'Come in.'

Al opened the door and, behind the desk, a man stood up. He was small, with dark hair and olive skin, and a name tag which read 'Mr M Bogazkale'. It was Mursili.

'Shut the door,' he said. 'Shut the door. We've got a lot to talk about.'

'Mursili—' Lexi said, still trying to take it all in. 'You made it.'

'The door? No.' Mursili looked confused. He stepped past her to close it. 'It was here already. I did escape Hattusa, though.' He reached down into the neck of his shirt and

pulled out a small golden object he was wearing on a chain. 'I tried to follow you. I thought you'd found a door. This piece broke off in my hand. It's from the tablet. When it's touching me, it says "wattar", and I can understand anyone. If I take it off, it says "home", but all I understand is Hittite and some Egyptian. I'm trying to learn your language though, so that I can speak it without my lucky charm.' He slipped the chain back into his shirt. 'I found you on the school roll on the intranet. Ms Sharp said she was expecting you back with a book, an old book.' He nodded towards the dictionary, which Al was holding with both hands.

He told them Bogazkale was the town in Turkey nearest to the ruins of Hattusa. He had found that by googling it.

'You have two names here,' he said. 'So Bogazkale is my second name. I also found this— ' He stepped behind his desk, reached for his computer mouse and clicked on something. 'Come around. Come here.'

'How do you know how to use a computer?' Lexi asked him. 'You're from the BC time.'

'I'm a librarian,' he said without looking up. 'We're very adaptable. We have to be. Besides, how hard is it? It's a board with letters set into it and a thing that moves an arrow. I made a Hittite water trolley from scratch when I was ten.' He shrugged, as if that must have been much harder, whatever it was. 'Also, I have this number.' He held up a business card with a phone number on it. 'Tech support.'

'But how did you get here before us?' Al took a step back and bumped into the arm of a chair. Where was the big hat? The Hittite robes? How did Mursili get to look exactly like a teacher-librarian? 'How come people already seem to know you?'

'I was hoping you two could explain that.' Mursili looked disappointed. 'You're the time travellers, after all. I'm surprised you do it if you don't know how it works.'

'I'm surprised we do it too,' Lexi said.

'You pushed—' Al stopped himself. It wasn't the time for an argument, even if Lexi had pushed the button.

'What did Lexi push? How do you do it exactly?' Mursili folded his arms. He looked more like a teacher-librarian than ever.

For a moment, neither of them spoke. Then Lexi pointed at the book. 'That's how we do it. It's a dictionary. A word lights up, then we follow it back into the past. And try not to get killed.'

Al put the dictionary down on Mursili's desk. 'We don't really know how it works. We've only done it twice. Most of the time, like now, it's just a normal old book. Then away we go. It's pretty surreal.'

'Or, in fact, completely real.' Mursili reached for his mouse. 'Let me show you.'

He clicked and a voice with a German accent started to speak. He was playing a video on YouTube, taken from a TV documentary about excavations at Hattusa in the early 20th century. A professor was talking about the tablets, and the Hittite version of the Battle of Ashkalon.

'But the Egyptian civilisation outlasted the Hittites,' he said. 'So the Egyptians wrote the history. Their records tell a different story. For thousands of years, we've thought the Egyptians won the Battle of Ashkalon, but it seems likely it was actually a Hittite victory, and these tablets are a big part of setting the record straight.' He cleared his throat. 'No one knew that in 1911, though, because no one could read the tablets.'

The video cut to a woman standing at a board with a pen. 'Everyone assumed it would be an Akkadian language,' she said, 'because those languages were spoken and written throughout the Middle East at the time. But nothing fitted. Then, on a tablet on the floor, we found what seemed to be a list and some instructions. And on the list was this.' She drew two characters on the board with her pen. 'These characters did exist elsewhere and they made the sounds "wat" and "tar". Wattar. It wasn't an Akkadian language at all. It was Indo-European and this was the word "water". More than 3,000 years ago. It's in the king's approved recipe for bread.'

Mursili clicked on the mouse again and the video stopped.

'So,' he said, 'you call it "water" and 3,000 years ago we called it "wattar". It's the same. It seems that's as far as records go, but everything I've read suggests that it began where our languages began, by the Caspian Sea, 6,000 years ago. There are no older words than "water".'

He brought photographs up on screen of the ruins of Hattusa and the tablets. The city fell, and the empire and language with it.

'We couldn't save Hattusa that day, but we saved the records,' he said to them. 'And you saved a life. You and that book saved a life. Even if you don't know exactly how it works, I want you to think very hard before giving it back.'

The dictionary was too fat for Al to fit into his backpack with everything he had to take home from school that afternoon, so he sat in the car with it resting on his lap. They had saved one life, and not saved at least one more. They had messed around with history, and so far history seemed hardly touched by it. He wondered who would have been in Mursili's office if Mursili wasn't there, but there was no way of knowing that now.

They were idling at traffic lights when their father noticed the sunlight glinting from the gold letters on the dictionary's cover.

'Could I—' He reached across and grabbed it as though he wasn't at the wheel of a car. 'Let me know if the lights change.'

He opened the dictionary and turned several pages.

'Dad, the lights have changed,' Lexi said from the back seat. 'Dad!'

He looked up. A car behind them honked and he closed the book.

He checked the rear-vision mirror. 'Right,' he said, giving the dictionary back to Al and letting the car move forward. 'Where did you get this? I think I've seen it before.'

'It's from the library,' Al said. Best to keep it simple.

'The school library?'

'You need to concentrate more on driving and less on being weird.'

The car was starting to veer across the lane. Their father flicked the indicator, pulled over to the side of the road and put on the handbrake.

'I think my father might have read this book once,' he said. 'Not long before he – went.'

Lexi leant forward. 'You think he vanished after reading that book?'

'Well, he disappeared. And I think he might have read the book,' their father said. 'But it's just a dictionary. Isn't it?'

The Curious Dictionary

Curious: adj. Odd, strange, inquisitive
[Lat, 'curiosus' inquisitive, cautious, from 'cura' care]

Dictionary: n. Book or series of books containing the words of a language or chosen subset of a language, usually alphabetical, with explanations of meanings and origins
[Med Lat, 'dictionarium', from 'dicere' to say]

& MORE

THE DICTIONARY SAT on Al's desk for another week, and then two. Sometimes at night he woke in the middle of a dream that had sent him deep into the past – fighting or being attacked or running through a forest – and he was sure the golden glow would be in his room again, but everything was dark.

Some days, he wished they had never found the dictionary. Lexi did too. But they *had* found it, and they had saved Mursili's life because of it, or that's how it looked. And now, every time either of them visited the library, he came out of his office to check if they had travelled back into history again.

'I wish he wouldn't keep going on about it,' Lexi said, after returning some books one lunchtime. 'It's easy for him to say we should do it. It wouldn't be his life on the line.'

'We'll see what the next word is,' Al said, hoping that counted as some kind of plan. 'It might be quite okay. Might be safe.'

'"Water" took us to two battles and two invasions.' As soon as Lexi said it, Al knew she was right. '"Water" only got to Britain because the Angles invaded and took it there. It only survived in Germania because they fought off the Romans. Words didn't end up in English because nice people thought they would be a good idea.'

But there was no decision to make, until the dictionary became active again.

That happened on a Tuesday, though they didn't know exactly when. Their father had picked them up from school and, when they got home, he went straight to the study to work on some townhouse plans.

As Al opened the door to his bedroom, he could hear humming. The dictionary was vibrating on his desk and light was pulsing from it. But the light wasn't coming from inside. It was coming from the cover, from the '&' symbol between "Walker" and "Fuller". In all the time he had spent thinking about the dictionary, he had never thought about that possibility. '&' wasn't even a word.

He wondered where it could take them and what they might see. He thought of suggesting to Lexi that they Google '&' to help them make the decision. He took Doug from his box, lifted the dictionary up carefully and carried it out to the back deck, where Lexi was about to start her homework.

'No,' she said when she saw him coming. 'We're not doing it. No more battles. I'm not going and you're not either. We could get killed.'

She stood up. Al put the dictionary down on the table and she reached out to stop him opening it. She put her hand on the cover, right over the title and on the glowing '&'.

'Lex—' Al said, but it was too late.

They were on their way into the past again.

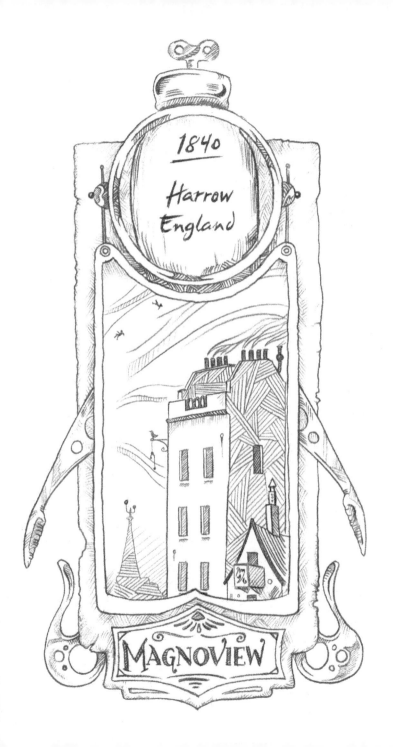

$\mathcal{T}$HERE WERE SMALL bumps, one after another, and a relatively short fall to daylight.

In the distance below them was a city with a haze of smoke over it, but they were falling towards woodland and farms, and a small town. There were playing fields, gardens and a tall orange brick building.

They landed downhill from it, though, outside a classroom in the grounds of a small school near the centre of the town. Through a window they could see a group of boys aged about seven reciting the alphabet as their teacher pointed to the letters on a blackboard.

But this alphabet didn't finish with Z. As the pointer worked its way along, the boys called out X, Y and Z, as expected but, after Z, the pointer fell on '&' and they all said something that slurred a little and might have been 'ampersand'.

'What happened?' Lexi said. 'We didn't even open the stupid book.'

'The button was on the cover.' Al undid the buckles on his leather satchel. 'It was the "and" symbol. I was going to tell you, but you—'

'What?' The word came out of Lexi's mouth sounding somewhere between a hiss and a shout. 'You mean *I* did this? I brought us here? I sent us off on another one of these idiot— '

Her hands were both clenched into fists.

Al worked hard not to laugh. 'Sounds like a fair summary of the situation.'

'Are you *trying* to send me psycho?'

'I think I'll leave that up to you. But let's see what we've got.' He reached into the satchel. 'There's only three this time.' He took out the peg that had lit up and showed it to her. He tried to focus on the place and time. 'I know there's a famous school here. It was certainly here in 1840, but I don't know if this is it.' He had always thought of Harrow School as bigger, grander. Perhaps it was the buildings further up the hill. '1840's good though. It's not a battle. Not here. You didn't drop us into a battle.'

'Give me time,' she said. 'I can do it. Two more pegs. All I want's the sword. I can't believe— '

A bell rang and the teacher dismissed the class.

'Do you think they activated the portal?' Lexi said. 'The teacher pointed to the "and" symbol and they said something.'

'That makes sense. It might be in the classroom. This could be easier than we thought. We could get out of here before anyone invades or arrests us or sets the place on fire.'

'Couldn't you have *told* me the thing was on the cover? You just bring it out and shove it at me and— ' She knew it wasn't his fault. 'Okay, but it's up to both of us to get us out of here. And through whatever's next. Let's talk to one of these kids.'

The students were on their way out of the building, ignoring Lexi and Al since they had ended up in the same school uniforms and simply looked like students from an older class.

One boy took a top from his pocket and crouched down to spin it. 'Excuse me,' Lexi said.

The boy stood up again. 'Butler Minor.'

'Butler Minor?' It didn't make any more sense when Lexi repeated it. 'What's a Butler Minor?'

'George was Butler Major, so I'm Butler Minor.' All he'd been doing was introducing himself. He looked them up and down. 'He was here years ago. He's much older than you and very clever. I don't think I know you.'

Lexi almost introduced herself in the usual way, but then she thought of something better. 'Hunter Major,' she said, 'and this is my brother, Hunter Minor.'

'Five minutes apart!' Al said before he could stop himself. 'That's not a Major and Minor thing. We tied for first. We're both Hunter Major.'

'I'm sorry,' Butler Minor said. 'There can't be two Hunter Majors. There are rules, you know.'

'You can be Loser Major instead then if you want,' Lexi said to Al, making an L sign with her thumb and finger. 'Now, Butler Minor—' There was no reason to say his name again, but it sounded so odd she couldn't help it. 'Tell us about that alphabet you were reciting. How did it finish?'

'Is this a test? This is lunchtime now.' He looked hesitant. 'We don't do tests at lunchtime. Lunchtime's for—'

'It's just a question,' she said. 'But you're allowed to answer it.'

'I'll give it whatever's required.' He clasped his hands behind his back and stood perfectly straight, as if to show Lexi she had his full attention. 'Is this one of those things you have to know before they let you go to the school on the hill?'

'Yes,' Lexi said. 'It is.' She wished the past could always be about interrogating seven-year-olds, rather than being charged at by Romans with swords or Normans with maces.

'How does the alphabet finish? What comes after Z?'

'And,' he said confidently. 'Per se And.'

'Now start at X,' Al said. It wasn't making sense yet.

Butler Minor thought about it. 'X, Y, Z and per se And. But the teachers have decided it's now all right to say the last bit as "ampersand", since that's how most people do it.'

'Good.' It wasn't much clearer as far as Al was concerned. 'Now tell us about the "per se" part.'

'Right.' Butler Minor cleared his throat, as if preparing to address a roomful of examiners. 'When we recite the alphabet, it's customary to use the expression "per se" – meaning "by itself" in Latin – before each letter which, in other circumstances, might be an entire word. There are three: A, I and &. So, we finish the alphabet by, after Z, saying "and per se And" or "ampersand".'

Lexi looked around. There were boys playing with balls or hitting each other or sitting talking. Butler Minor had said 'ampersand' twice, but there was no sign of a portal.

'The symbol is from the Latin "et" meaning "and".' Butler Minor was going for bonus points now. 'The two letters were sometimes written joined together, in a form called a ligature. Printers did it, but so did people as far back as the Romans, and those two joined letters became the symbol we use today.'

'Really? The Romans?' The last thing Lexi wanted was another battle in a muddy forest in Germania.

As a cloud passed in front of the sun, Al noticed a glow coming from the classroom. He looked through the window and saw that the '&' on the board had turned a golden colour and was pulsing with light.

'Got it.' He pointed it out to Lexi.

'Thanks, Butler Minor,' she said, as she followed Al to the steps. 'You'll do well up the hill.'

The classroom door was open and, as they got there, they realised something different was happening this time. Golden light was coming from a number of points around the room – from desks and piles of books and charts on the walls. Wherever there was an ampersand, it seemed to be glowing.

'It's too much,' Lexi said. 'It's a distraction. And they're all just ampersands. None of them's like one of those buttons. Where's the "more"? Also, Butler Minor took "ampersand" all the way back to the Romans. We know the story already. We've got there in one step.'

'Maybe the next one takes us to the printers, and then we've got the Romans and then we go home.'

'Or maybe there's something else going on.' She was looking around the room, trying to see past all the glowing ampersands to an '& more'.

Butler Minor had followed them into the room.

'Oh dear,' he said to Al. 'Do you have food in your bag? You know that's against the rules. I think you have a mouse.'

Doug's nose was poking out from Al's satchel, sniffing, sniffing – mould, closed up boy-smell, fear and, somewhere not far away, cheese. He tried to pull himself out, but Al pushed him back down.

'Is there anything different?' Al asked Butler Minor. 'Anything that wasn't here before the bell rang?'

'Yes,' he said. 'The mouse, which really needs to be dealt with. And that.'

He was pointing to a banner on the wall that read, 'The clue is in the cloth.' It was embroidered, with the writing done as though it was a continuous line of ribbon, ending in a squiggle with an image of a needle sewn into the fabric.

'Stand back,' Al told him. 'And it's a rat, not a mouse. Try not to be so smug, by the way. Examiners don't like that.'

He and Lexi crossed the room. In the eye of the needle was a tiny glowing button with '& more' on it.

'Right, yes, well,' Butler Minor said, his cheeks turning pink. 'George says that to me all the time. I thought— '

Lexi touched the button to open the portal as Al took out the peg. He locked it in place, turned the key and the air between them and Butler Minor grew hazy.

1124

Winchester
England

MAGNOVIEW

L EXI AND AL lurched as they fell, and then hit a bump and turbulence. Once they passed through that there was a sheer drop, then a swerve, then a clear fall.

There were fields below them and a town with a tangle of streets, a castle and a long building casting the biggest shadow of all. They fell towards the streets, though, to a yard behind a building and they landed on a bale of wool.

'Is this the printers?' Lexi said when they checked the peg. '1124. This is raw wool we've landed on. Like straight off the sheep. I've seen it on *The Farmer Wants a Wife.*'

'Does everything you know come from reality TV?' Al looked around the yard. There was a scrawny dog asleep in the far corner and an empty cart against one wall. 'The clue is in the cloth.' Maybe that banner meant more than they'd realised. From inside the building he could hear clicking and clacking and thumping. 'What if this is a factory, turning the wool into cloth? The banner got us here, but now we have to find the printers.'

Lexi checked what she was wearing. There were no weapons or any sign that she was going to have to fight. She had a gown that went most of the way to her ankles and sleeves that flared at the wrists. Al was in a shirt, a tunic with a belt around it and striped leggings. They both had slippers

made from pieces of leather tied together with leather cords.

'Nice leggings,' she said to him. 'You look like a bee this time, instead of a chicken.'

'I'm over with leggings!' How come Lexi always ended up with better clothes than him? 'We look kind of rich, or not poor, anyway. I think we're doing okay this 12th century, as long as no one shoots another king in front of us. Winchester's where they were going to take us 24 years ago, wasn't it?' To Winchester and to justice – that was what Walter Tyrell had said.

'Let's go,' Lexi said. 'I don't want to think about him.'

The door to the building was open and inside were two men standing in wooden troughs, pounding their feet methodically into something that sounded wet. One man looked over as they appeared.

'Are you here with wool, sir?' he said to Al. 'The classer's down with one of the bishop's flocks. He might be a while.'

'That's all right,' Al said. 'We're not in a hurry. We've got to do business with the printer as well.'

'Printer? Right— ' The man frowned. 'Are we expecting you, sir? Mister— '

'Hunter. Alastair Hunter.' The full name sounded better, more like someone you'd call 'sir'. 'I think my father talked to someone here about our flock.'

'Very good, sir. We'd be very happy to have your family's wool here.' The man stopped pounding and leant on a beam in front of him. 'I'm Godwin Walker and this here's Harold Fuller.'

'Walker and Fuller!' Lexi said. It couldn't be a coincidence. 'You're the ones who started *Walker & Fuller's Curious Dictionary?*'

'I don't know any dictionary, miss.' He stood up from the beam he'd been resting against. 'I don't go starting things. I haven't been in trouble for years.'

'You're Walker and Fuller, though?'

'Just look at us.' He said it as if it was an answer.

'What do you mean?' Al said.

'Walker, Fuller, Tucker – it's all the same,' the other

man, Harold Fuller, said. 'You haven't seen your wool worked on, then?'

He stepped out of the trough and his bare feet were cracked and swollen. He bathed them in a bucket of water and wiped them with a rag.

'That there's fuller's earth,' he said, pointing down into the trough, at the wool mixed with clay. 'It takes the oil out of the wool when you walk it in. The walking also mats the fibres and makes the wool thicker, or fuller. That's why those of us who do this end up as Walker or Fuller.'

'Or Tucker,' Godwin said.

'Or Tucker. Same thing. Same job, different name for it. The wool spreads out and you have to keep tucking it back in. Lots of Tuckers around here.'

Godwin stepped out and sat down on a stool. He cleaned his feet, too. Their skin was pale and puffy and the cracks ran deep.

'So, you've got your names just because of your jobs?' Lexi said.

'There's a lot of us with names from wool,' Harold said. 'Nothing wrong with that. We can't all be Bishops or Knights, or even Hunters, though you look like you've done well for hunters. There's Jack Weaver and William Dyer here for a start.'

Obviously this Walker and this Fuller hadn't started the *Curious Dictionary*. Lexi began to wonder if their visit to 1124 wasn't about printers at all, or the ampersand. Perhaps they were here to learn that Walker and Fuller were one and the same. She looked around the room. There were several troughs on the floor and wool was spread out on racks, but there was no sign of a glowing '& more' button.

'Maybe we're going to the origins of the dictionary,' she said to Al. 'We've done the ampersand, now we know what Walker and Fuller mean, and the only thing left on the cover is where it says "Curious Dictionary". Maybe we need to find something to take us there.'

'Okay,' Al said. 'But I'm not sure they've got dictionaries in 1124.'

'So let's see what they do have. If it's "Walker" and "Fuller" that we were supposed to hear, the portal's been activated somewhere, so we should— '

At that moment, something hit Al's bag with a thump. It knocked him forwards, but he grabbed a post to steady himself. A cat yowled and tore at the top of the bag. Inside, Doug scrambled madly for safety.

'All right, all right,' Godwin said, stepping forward. He took the cat in both hands and pulled it away. Its claws hung on and it yowled again. 'All right! Let go.'

The cat twisted around, its claws came free and it dropped from his hands and ran under a trough.

'Mouser,' he said. 'We get a lot of mice coming in to nest in the wool. I don't know what you've got in that bag, but maybe you'd be better waiting out the front.' He pointed to a door. 'We'll let your father know you're here, the moment he arrives.'

'Okay, the portal's got to be somewhere,' Lexi said quietly as Al pushed the door open. 'Let's take the tour. Let's tell them we're interested in seeing what happens to Dad's wool.'

As the door closed behind them, Doug slid out from between two books. He sniffed, to check that he was safe. Right now, this place had only two smells – rat sweat and wee. At least Al's sketchpad had soaked up most of it.

In the next room Lexi and Al met William Dyer and Tom Lincoln, who were dyeing wool green. Tom took his name from the place his family came from. There was also a Tom Johnson in the workshop, and having two names helped to tell them apart.

'It's the names,' Lexi said, as they left the dyeing room. 'That's what this one's all about. It's the origin of family names.'

Neither of them had ever thought of family names as being anything but family names, passed on from one generation to the next, forever. But it made sense that, like everyday words, they had started somewhere.

They realised they had come to the time when family names were beginning in English, and when your name might say what you did, or where you were from, or who your father was. Each one had its own meaning, other than simply identifying a family. At some stage in the history of their family, perhaps 900 years before their time, they had probably had an ancestor who was a hunter.

'And that's all great,' Al said, as Lexi took him through it, 'but how does it get us to the portal? "The clue is in the cloth" – where is something like that?'

There was a bench near them with samples of dyed fabric, spools of thread and a box of things that appeared to be combs, but other than that the hallway was empty. A rhythmic clicking noise was coming from a room on the right.

'What about places?' Lexi said. 'We move around a bit from one time to the next. The last clue was in the cloth and it brought us here, to a place making cloth. We've found Walker and Fuller, so this one seems to be about names, and one thing we've learnt is that some people are named after the place they come from. What about a name that might take us somewhere?'

Al didn't have a better idea. They went back to Tom Lincoln and got him to talk about his home town. Nothing happened. They asked about other people with names that came from places. Robert Farnham sold cloth in the shop at the front of the workshop, but nothing he said about Farnham made a portal appear.

He mentioned Edward Newbury who worked for Isaac Goldsmith across the road, but Edward Newbury said Newbury was too new for there to be much to talk about.

'I'm not sure this is it,' Al said to Lexi, while they pretended to look at brooches. 'We're getting nowhere. Maybe we have to go back to Walker and Fuller. Or look for a printer.'

'Or maybe not.'

Tucked next to the gold pin of a brooch on the tray in front of Lexi was a paperclip. She picked it up and set it down by itself where Al could see it.

He nodded. 'Yes, I like that one,' he said.

They heard the door open behind them and in came a customer.

'Henry Norwich,' the man said to Edward as he stepped up to the counter. 'I was here earlier talking to Isaac about a locket.'

'Oh, yes,' Edward said. 'He put something aside for you to look at.'

He reached into a drawer below the counter and removed a leather pouch. He opened it and placed the locket into Henry Norwich's hand. The golden light pulsing from it made his whole hand glow.

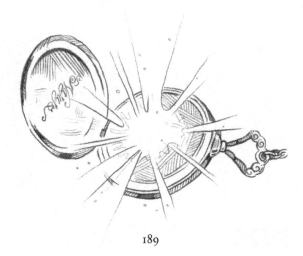

'I'm not sure,' Henry Norwich said. 'It's for my daughter.'

'Perhaps my sister could show you what it might look like on her?' Al said.

'Yes.' Henry Norwich looked at Lexi. 'Please, it would be very helpful if you'd try it on.'

He reached his hand out and, as Lexi took the locket, she could feel the portal opening up.

'Let's take a step back,' Al said, 'so that Mr Norwich can see how it'll look across a room.'

The peg was already in his hand.

460

Northwic
East
Angle Lands

MAGNOVIEW

*T*HERE WAS A shudder, a patch of smooth air and a long clear fall. Then Lexi and Al both felt sick and started to sweat.

When the air cleared, there was a land of forests and fields below them and, far in the distance, the sea on three sides. The rush of cold air on their faces helped the sick feeling start to pass. As they fell they could see the bends of a river, and then a cluster of buildings on one of its banks. There was nothing grand or imposing, and it didn't seem like a place of much importance. At least there didn't seem to be a war going on.

They landed on the edge of the village, in a sty outside a cottage made of mudbrick and timber. One of the pigs looked up from a trough and looked away again, as if people fell from the sky all the time. Doug tumbled out of Al's bag and landed with a *plop*.

'Oh, great,' Lexi said. 'Mud.' She could feel it oozing through her clothes. 'Or worse than mud – unless the pigs have a separate toilet! Whose idea was this? Why couldn't we land a couple of metres away?'

Doug climbed up Al's leg, found a dry patch on his leggings and wiped most of the mud off before climbing to Al's shoulder and scurrying back into the sack he was carrying.

'Oh, good, I've been waiting for you,' a voice said from inside.

Al and Lexi reached for their belts in case they were armed, but there was nothing there. They were wearing rough clothes that probably hadn't had much shape to them before they had become half-covered in mud. It was hard to work out who they were supposed to be.

The door of the cottage opened and a man came out. He had a white beard and white hair around the edges of his balding head.

'Caractacus,' he said. 'We met in Angeln, 30 years ago. You were hunting "water".'

Neither of them spoke. It felt like something no one was supposed to know. Al stood up and took a step away from him.

'It's all right,' Caractacus said. 'Nothing too dramatic happens here. It's already happened. Norwich, 460. Northwic, the Angles call it. Don't bother to check the peg. Come inside and I'll take you into everything.'

'What do you know—' Lexi stopped herself before she mentioned the peg. 'We're filthy. You don't want us in there.'

'It's the Dark Ages.' Caractacus pulled the door fully open and waved for them to go in. 'Everything's filthy. Inside's filthy. We don't even have the word "filthy", because it's just what everything is. But don't get me beginning with that one.'

He was already beginning, and he kept muttering to himself about the failings of his time as he followed them inside.

The room was far larger than it looked from the outside, almost impossibly large. Perhaps it was the darkness that created that effect, or the smoke. In the stone hearth, a fire was spluttering under a heavy metal pot that hung from the ceiling. The smoke smelt of wood and candles and a dozen things Lexi and Al couldn't pin down. There were shelves with devices and tools on them, as well as boxes and piles of books and scrolls. It was like a junk shop and a mad scientist's laboratory and, at the same time, quite a lot like the pig sty outside.

There were two cups and a jug on the table, and Caractacus fetched a third cup from a shelf and poured them each a drink. Neither Lexi nor Al planned to drink it. Caractacus was far too weird for that.

'It's safe,' he said. 'Safer than the water. You'd worry about that kind of thing, wouldn't you? Sickening water? You're from after the 1850s?' Neither of them answered. It felt like a trap, or at least a trick question. How could anyone in 460 know they were from after the 1850s? '1854? Doctor John Snow? First discovery of diseases carried in water?'

Caractacus was right and Al knew it. 'The Broad Street pump in London. There was cholera. How have you heard about that?'

'Well done.' Caractacus was pleased. 'A historian. Well done. That'll be useful.' He took a good look at both of them. 'All right. This is where it begins. The *Curious Dictionary*. This room, this century, with me. I've met every hunter. You all come through here, if you pass the tests. And you've passed the tests, so this is your official briefing. Now, what century are you from? Late 20th? Or 21st?'

Lexi and Al looked at each other. 'Early 21st,' Lexi said. It didn't seem like much to give away, since his guess was already close enough. And he had fixed her arm in Angeln. He had been good to them there.

Caractacus started by explaining that Britain had fallen to the Angles and Saxons one town and fort and kingdom after another during the mid-5th century. The British languages were already being lost at a pace too fast to save them.

'But I have this,' he said.

He fetched a box of scrolls from a shelf, and then a box that had bags of powder, bunches of leaves and jars of metal filings. He pulled out a scroll, unwound the first part of it and showed it to them.

'It's mostly Greek,' he said, 'and if you read Greek, it's knowledge. It's the knowledge I need, and the procedures,

to make the book of the language that will become English. A book that will last and change as it needs to, and hold the language in just the right grip,' he said. 'In your time, that book is called *Walker & Fuller's Curious Dictionary*. You know that now, and you know that Walker and Fuller are just part of its disguise. I was Vortigern's man in the latter days of the Britons – you know that too – and then I served Ambrosius, then Uther Pendragon. Their father was High Lord before Vortigern.'

Al took a sip from his cup without thinking about it. The liquid that fizzed in his mouth tasted of apple and spices.

The scroll hung loose in Caractacus's hands. He set it on the table without rolling it and its fabric fell into folds.

'They'll come to write the story differently – the future English, I mean – with Uther's boy a hero and my appearance by another name, but the Britons have fallen, the boy is a bandit in the west who steals from the Saxons and hides in the forest, and no power in my scrolls can exert itself over that. But if I save English – if I build something that will keep the new language alive and grow with it – this might not happen again.'

He looked at them to see if they understood, but they were from too far away for that, too many centuries.

'This isn't like your time,' he told them. 'There are barely a thousand of us across these islands who can read and write, and that's not enough. Not enough for us to have a memory, not enough for words to have the force they should, not enough for knowledge to build on knowledge. And we haven't all been speaking the same language anyway. At the start of this century, there were dozens of British languages across the country. Some of them had only a handful of people who could write them. We were never going to defeat the Angles and Saxons like that.'

The fire started spitting and there was smoke coming from the pot. Caractacus moved quickly to a bench, where he put on thick gloves and picked up a pair of long tongs.

'Wolframite,' he said, pointing the tongs back towards Lexi and Al, or, in fact, at the boxes on the table. 'It's the third jar from this end. Take the second-smallest spoon and bring me a level spoonful.'

Al looked into the box. There were six metal spoons of different sizes on a ring. He found the second-smallest, scooped it into the jar of dark crushed crystals and tapped the excess off until it was level.

'Quickly, quickly,' Caractacus said.

Al held his other hand under the spoon as he crossed the dirt floor. Caractacus reached into the smoking pot with the tongs and lifted out a cup of molten metal.

'In there,' he said, turning to bring it to Al.

Al could feel the heat as he tipped the crystals in. Caractacus set the cup back into the pot and watched it closely.

'Impurities,' he said, after close to a minute's silence.

He put the tongs down and picked up another tool from his bench. It was a fine metal basket on a wire handle half as long as his arm. He scooped it into the pot twice, then tapped it on the side. He picked the tongs up again, lifted the cup and swirled it around without taking it out of the pot. He set it down and waited until the surface was still. Then he lifted the cup all the way out of the pot and held it steadily above two bricks that were clamped together and standing on their ends on the floor.

It was only when he poured the bright liquid metal that Lexi and Al could see there was a small hole where the bricks met. The metal was running down into a mould, and Caractacus kept pouring until it was full to the top.

'Are you a wizard of some kind?' Lexi said. The wizards in movies did exactly what he had just been doing.

'What I am is what I am.' Caractacus's eyes were still on the mould and the level of the metal. 'And there is only one of me, so a name is not essential. You're not wrong, though. I will be written as a wizard in some places, but I am a seeker, a tracker of knowledge. I am a hunter. I am the first hunter, and you are hunters too. But we have been chosen to live an unwritten history, so you won't see me called a word hunter.'

He set the empty cup down on the hearth, put the tongs back on the bench and turned to face Lexi and Al.

'No one in your time must know what you do,' he said. 'You understand that, don't you? For the next thousand years – no, more than that – they would burn you as witches. Even after that, even in your time, be aware that, as the only people who can travel to the past, you will be targets the moment anyone knows. Some people would do anything to have the dictionary, if they knew there was such a thing. They would use it to change the past so that the present changed to their own advantage. Money, countries – it could give them almost anything.'

He checked the mould again. The metal was cooling just as it was supposed to. He lifted the mould and placed it carefully in a bucket of water.

Lexi and Al both wanted Caractacus to say something different, something that meant it was all less serious and less dangerous than he had just made it sound.

'It's an astounding gift you've been given,' he said. 'Think of what you'll see, what you've already seen. It's also a terrible burden. I know that. But you're better than most. Most think they've got the answer to this one in Harrow or Winchester and do a lot more wandering around before they get here. So, I'll show you more. The more you know, the better you'll be. And the safer you'll be. You ask if I'm a wizard even though you come from a time that knows too much to believe in them. What I'm doing might look like magic to some people, but what do you think it is?'

'Science?' Al said, though he wasn't sure it was the right answer. It felt like one of those questions teachers ask when they have only one word in mind and you know you'll never get it.

'Good.' Caractacus looked pleased. 'Well done. "Science" is a good word for it, for what I've just done and for what's behind the dictionary. The dictionary is more complicated than anything you've just seen, but what makes it is knowledge. Knowledge your time doesn't have, which is why it might seem like magic. People call something magic when they can't explain it. That's why we call everything magic now. And why you'll end up calling this rather dreadful time the Dark Ages. And why some fool 600 years from now will end up calling me a wizard and giving me the name of a mad Welshman who had his head scrambled by the Saxon wars – but that's another story.'

There always seemed to be another story. That was the trouble with knowing so much. Caractacus had to continually remind himself that the word hunters didn't need – and didn't want – to know everything.

He explained that he had enough knowledge from earlier times to start the dictionary and make it curious – a seeker of words, a holder of language – but after that it had to build itself. The ampersand, Walker and Fuller, and the plush deep-red cover had all come along in the centuries ahead, keeping the dictionary looking never quite in fashion, but always like a work of authority from a time just past.

But Caractacus knew it wasn't perfect. He was missing some scrolls and had had to make approximations. Some worked well enough, but others led to weaknesses.

The dictionary's contents weren't stable, not all the time anyway. He told Lexi and Al that it was like a landslide or an earthquake – one unstable word changed the balance of the whole collection, and other words slipped too, one after another, dozens of them, sometimes a hundred or more over just a few years. Then balance was restored, perhaps even for years, but new words would always come along and eventually it would tip again. Caractacus had yet to find the knowledge he needed to fix that. For now, and possibly forever, the way around it was the word hunters.

He explained that, while some words fade out of use naturally, living words might be lost from the language if not pinned down by word hunters and their pegs at each stage of their evolution.

'That mightn't seem like much,' he said, 'but you haven't lived through the 5th century. I've seen languages lost. I know it can happen, and I know what's at stake when it does. I'm one of the last living speakers of the language of the Iceni, and once a language goes everything goes. Culture, history, the meaning of the place. There'll be nothing left of the Iceni soon but a few gold coins and a story of a warrior queen. That's the price of invasion. And it'll keep happening, all over the world. That's why languages need to do whatever they can to keep their power. Writing, reading – they can be crucial.'

Something in the hearth caught his eye. He went over and prodded the fire with a poker.

'Think about your country.' The flames rose and he stepped back. 'Think about your time. If only a thousand people could read and you weren't two of them, and you never met anyone who could, what would you know? What could you do? Which of your fancy machines would help you? Which of them could you work out how to use? Which of them could have been invented in the first place? Language is fragile. It's always fragile and more fragile than I hope you'll ever know. If too many words are lost, the Dark

Ages will come back. And look at it.' He gave a sweep of his arm, indicating the dark room and the dirt. 'Mud inside, mud outside and I live with pigs. Is that what you want? The pigs are the best bit.'

He picked the scroll up from the table and started rolling it, trying to keep the ends neat.

'I lived with kings,' he said, 'but this is where I need to be now. Those kings are dead and their sons are kings of nothing. Kings in stories that haven't been told yet, but nothing more. Someone needs to do what I'm doing. It's a job in the service of people who aren't yet born, not in the service of kings. That's a reason to take risks, to fight Normans and Romans and whoever it takes.'

He was looking at Lexi as he made the point. She felt he could see inside her and see everything.

'Perhaps you'd like a turn,' he said to her, indicating the box of powders and minerals. 'A level number two of wolframite.'

She scooped the ground crystals up and levelled the spoon. Caractacus slipped his hands back into the thick gloves and picked up the tongs again. He lowered them into the pot and lifted up another cup of molten metal, then turned carefully to face Lexi and nodded for her to drop the wolframite in. The crystals hit the metal and vanished. Caractacus returned the cup to the pot and swirled it around.

'Young man,' he said to Al, 'perhaps you would glove yourself and attend to the scooping. You saw me do that before? Skimming the impurities off?'

He nodded towards a shelf, where Al found a pair of stiff gloves too big for his hands. He put them on anyway and tried to close one hand around the scoop, but ended up needing both to pick it up and hold it steady. Heat rose from the pot as he leaned over it. He could see something dark and crusty on the surface of the metal and he lowered the basket to scoop it up. He tapped the handle on the side of the pot, as Caractacus had done, and the impurities fell out.

Caractacus lifted the cup and crouched down to pour the metal into another mould on the floor. He set the empty cup down on the hearth, picked up the mould and lowered it carefully into a bucket of water.

'Words come to life by chance,' he said, as he stood up, 'and they can die by it too. You'll see that, the more you do. But they can also die if they're not looked after, if they're not held in place. That's what we do. That's what the pegs do. We don't need to make words, it turns out. Humans are great at that. That's what's exciting. You've done "hello"? If the dictionary's right, can you imagine how you would greet each other in your time if Rollo's brother Gurim had become Duke of Normandy instead?'

'Hello' seemed like a long time ago to Lexi and Al. They had zigzagged across 3,000 years since then, lurching from one time to another. Fig Tree Pocket in the 21st century was starting to feel no more nor less real than anywhere else.

Al noticed that the last of the sick feeling he had had when they arrived was gone. Perhaps the drink Caractacus gave them had helped.

'Why does it feel the way it does?' he asked. 'Moving from one time period to another?'

'You're all right now, though? Better than when you landed?'

'Yes.' Al couldn't remember having said that he felt off when they landed.

'Here's how it works,' Caractacus said. 'You can't travel between time periods on nothing. There's something that carries you, something built on words. It has a physical force but it has no name, because it's known only to us. Some hunters 200 years before your time called it a "miasma", which is a kind of fog. In the 20th century they called it a "plasma" or a "vector", but these are all names of other things and its name doesn't really matter. What matters is what it does and, to a lesser extent, how it does it.'

He explained that the path between times was not smooth. The speed was not constant, events could put bumps in the way and any move back in the history of a word that would take them to another country would be felt as a big lurch sideways.

He went to another corner of the room where scrolls lay in rows on a shelf and he worked his way along until he found the one he wanted. He pulled it out, brought it back to the table and unrolled it. It showed a timeline, with notes added and arrows pointing all over the place.

But the line wasn't straight and sometimes it wasn't just one line. It was the history of English.

He took them through it backwards, era by era, from the duelling dictionaries of Webster and Johnson, to the playwrights around 1600, to the increase in the trade of words and goods that had occurred before then. Then came the printing press, the Normans, King Alfred. It was a complicated story, and Caractacus seemed at home with every detail of it.

'I hope you're remembering this,' Lexi said to Al and, mostly, he was.

'Of course, Old English was a very different English from the English you speak,' Caractacus said, having arrived almost at his own time. 'You'd hardly understand early English at all. *Fysrt forth gewat, flota waes on ythum, bat under beorge.*' They looked at him blankly. It sounded totally garbled. 'It means something like, "Time went on, the boat was on the sea, the boat was under the cliff." You could probably almost understand the last bit, "bat under beorge" – the boat under the cliff. Except of course "cliff" doesn't turn up until later, with the Vikings.'

'So how come we can understand people in different times, and they can understand us?' Lexi had remembered one of the things they had wanted to know. 'In the New Forest, when King William's shot, wouldn't they all be speaking a kind of French? We heard them in English. English pretty much like ours.'

'Ah, yes, the pegs do that.' Caractacus nodded. 'Stay near the pegs and you'll hear everything in your language and anyone you're talking to will hear you in theirs. There's a mechanism inside, a translation engine. It's quite clever.'

'What about now?' Al said. 'Are we using the pegs to understand you?'

'Me?' Caractacus laughed. 'No. You don't need them here. I'm speaking your English, or English—' He turned to Lexi, and tried to remember the exact wording. 'English pretty much like yours. I listen to everything every word hunter tells me. This won't be the last time we meet, you know. I'll be learning from you while you're learning from me.' That seemed to send him off down a new track. 'So, early 21st century. Do you still have movies, and do you still call them that?'

'Yes.' It was the second part of the question Lexi found odd. 'Why would we call them anything else?'

'Well, they're never going to get their own name now then, are they?' Caractacus shook his head. 'More than a hundred years and – I don't want to call it lazy – but you do realise "movies" is just short for "moving pictures"? And don't come at me with "film" because that's just a thin layer or skin.' He shrugged. 'I suppose it's also a good thing when language adapts, but there is a thrill with a new word. I was hoping for a new word. Next question – do you use computers, and what do you use them for?'

'Yes.' Al tried to think how best to explain it. 'Computers were originally the size of a room and didn't do much – just maths, I think – but now some of them fit in your hand and they can tell you pretty much anything. Do you know about the internet?'

'Internet?' Caractacus thought about it. 'That sounds like a prefix and a suffix waiting for somewhere to go.'

Al tried to work out what to say next. The internet was just part of life. No one ever needed it explained to them. 'It's

an electronic way of accessing billions of pages of information, or sending messages around the world instantly.'

'To find things out, you can use something like Google,' Lexi added.

'Google.' Caractacus said it as though he'd been let in on a secret. 'I like that. I think it's brand new. You're going to have to spell it for me.' He wrote it down letter by letter on a loose piece of parchment. 'And what, exactly, is a Google?'

'Just "Google",' Lexi said. 'No "a". It's a search engine.'

'Excellent.' He wrote that down too. 'Now, tell me about this search engine. Is it bigger than a bread box? Does it run on wheels or tracks? What does it do when it arrives at water?'

Lexi laughed. 'It's not that kind of engine. Al, phone.'

She reached out. Al took his phone from his sack and handed it to her.

'In the 21st century, this is a phone,' she told Caractacus. 'A telephone. It's come a long way since Mr Edison and Mr Bell.'

She pressed a button and the *Doctor Who* theme played as the phone turned on. Caractacus flinched, then leant in for a closer look.

'Is that radio?' he said. 'I've heard of radio.'

'I think we should sit down,' Lexi said. 'This'll take a while.'

It took hours to explain technology in the early 21st century. Caractacus made extensive notes as they talked, underlining any new words or new meanings of words. Al took him through the functions of his phone, or at least the ones he could show without a signal. For the first time in his life, Caractacus had his photo taken.

He gazed at the picture as if it was something miraculous, and then he stepped outside with Lexi and took a photo of his fattest pig.

'One thing I've wondered,' Lexi said without thinking it through, 'is why any photos we take in the past are gone when we get home.'

'You're asking me?' Caractacus said, accidentally taking a photo of his own knees as he shut the door on their way back inside. 'Not long ago, I thought a search engine was probably a train with a light on it.'

While the others were outside, Al had been copying Caractacus's English language timeline into one of his notebooks.

'Could you tell me what these crosses are next to the 5th century?' he said. 'And what this word is?' He had his finger on the scroll.

Caractacus put the camera down. 'Nausea. That's what every word hunter feels going through the Dark Ages. I always find it's best to have a fizzy drink on hand.'

'What about things beyond the timeline?' Al said. 'This doesn't go way into the past. There's a big bump and a grinding noise at the fall of Hattusa.'

'Oh, Hattusa.' Caractacus frowned. 'Water, yes? Wattar? I think what you felt is the thing you'll end up calling the Bronze Age Collapse. Terrible time. You should find a Google for it when you have the chance. Some very, very old words will take you there, and I'm not sure that there's a way through. There's language behind it, but almost none of it written. It's another knowledge crash, like the Dark Ages. They keep happening. That's exactly my point.' He turned away from the table, and looked towards the burnt-out fire and the metal pot. 'I think we should be ready now.'

He indicated they should follow and led them over to the hearth, where he lifted the two moulds from the water and set them on the bench. He put his gloves on and opened the clips on one of the moulds. He lifted one brick away and tipped the other onto his hand. A gleaming, silver-coloured peg fell out.

'Yes, ready,' he said, tossing it around in the glove. 'I don't think knowledge is everything, but it's drastic to lose it. Some other things matter too. Food, kindness. But food is easier to come by or grow or catch if you have the knowledge to do it, and it's much easier to be kind if you're not fighting for food. Or it should be.' He turned the second peg out into his glove. 'Every so often we lose a thousand years of knowledge, you know. A thousand or two. And then we have to find it all again, and we never quite manage it. We find more, but pieces stay lost. This book – the making of this book – can you do that in your time with all your spectacular devices? You can't, can you? The knowledge was lost. Almost lost.'

He took a rag and rubbed at the pegs so that any final impurities fell away. They gleamed in the dim light. He found a box on a shelf and took out levers, two locking mechanisms and some tiny tools. He reached into a pocket of his robe, took out a lens, wiped it and tucked it into one eye socket. It made his eye look larger.

'So that's what you're doing as word hunters. It's not just keeping a word here and there alive, keeping people saying "hello" to each other.' He attached levers to one peg, and adjusted them until they worked smoothly. 'It's about a language living and growing, and having the thousands of words it needs to have for knowledge to be passed on and built upon.'

He took some time to fit a red-jewelled locking mechanism and key, and then picked up the second set of levers and slipped them into place on the other peg. He clipped a locking mechanism over the top and secured it.

'I'm going to show you what I mean about knowledge,' he said, as he tested the two pegs. One of the keys moved in and out smoothly, but the other stuck a little. He took a bottle of liquid and wiped a drop on the key. He checked it again and it passed freely in and out of the lock. 'The knowledge I use to make the book comes from Alexandria in Egypt, from the greatest library of the ancient world. It needs a special peg, there and back. You can only go there with me. Access to the library can't fall into the wrong hands. So, the pegs are made of different metals entirely. The wolframite provides tungsten. It's unusually strong. These ones are solid. There's no translation … ' He paused as he looked for the right word. 'App?'

He slipped one peg into a pocket and kept the other in his hand.

'There will be some danger,' he said. 'You must do exactly as I say.' He could see that Lexi wasn't happy. 'So far I've brought everyone back and I'm not planning to change that now.'

'And after that we go straight home?' she said. It seemed like the best deal she could make. She was sure Caractacus would be the only way to the Norwich portal, and Alexandria didn't seem to be optional.

'That's right.'

He took a box from a shelf and lifted out a leather bag. In it, wrapped in cloth, was something that looked like an old perfume bottle. It had a tube that dipped down into liquid and there was a bulb attached at the top. He pointed the bottle at the wall and squeezed the bulb. A green mist sprayed out and, on one of the beams in the wall, a portal lit up.

'Come closer,' he said, as he drove the peg in.

THE THREE OF them lurched sideways, then fell through thinner air, faster and faster. Caractacus seemed to glide like a great bearded bird, his hair and robes flapping behind him.

Once their view of the ground cleared, it was night. A city was on fire and they were falling towards the middle of it. Ships in the port had rolled onto their sides and were burning, the docks were ablaze and the wind was pushing in from the sea and driving the fire down the streets, into grain stores and palaces and the great Library of Alexandria.

As they fell, the heat rose to meet them and ash blew past.

'That's it,' Caractacus shouted over the roar of the wind. 'That's knowledge burning – books and scrolls. Follow me.'

He tilted his body to the side, swung one arm back and the other forward, and banked to the right. It was the first time Lexi and Al had any idea they could follow anything, or have any effect on their fall. They copied his moves and slid across the sky after him.

Caractacus was aiming for the one corner of the library that wasn't burning, and he brought them to a smooth landing on the steps outside. Around them, people were giving up the fight and running, shouting at each other in a language Lexi and Al couldn't understand.

'No app,' Al said, as much to himself as to Lexi.

'Follow me in,' Caractacus said. 'There's one door that's still working.'

Ash fell from the sky like grey and black leaves, drifting down when the heat left it. It was all over the ground, skidding across the steps as the wind gusted.

'All the knowledge in the known world,' he said. 'This is the only place it was brought together. I have no idea how great my century might have been if this fire hadn't happened. Or your century.'

Ash fell on the back of Lexi's hand. She could just make out the shapes of letters before wind folded it over and crumpled it.

Caractacus moved up the steps of the building. There was a booming sound as the roof of a nearby grain store collapsed and sparks shot up into the sky.

'Caesar did this,' Caractacus shouted without turning around. 'Julius Caesar. He meant to burn the ships, but the wind changed.'

He led them past a stone column and around the corner to a small wooden door that was already open. The passage inside was dark, but clear of smoke. They followed him in.

'This is a mission too,' Caractacus said, as they made their way along the passage. 'Every time we come here, the dictionary is at risk. There are certain scrolls we must take back to make the dictionary and everything that goes with it. Once we have them, we grab everything we can.'

At the end of the passage he pushed a door open, and they found themselves in an abandoned kitchen. Beyond it was a dining room, with meals still on the tables and smashed plates on the floor. People had been eating here minutes before. A scroll lay on one table, partly unrolled, and Al grabbed it as they ran past.

'Leave that,' Caractacus shouted. 'I've looked at it before. Other things are more important. It's Aristotle writing about comedy. There are bound to be copies somewhere else.'

Ahead of them in the building, there was a crashing sound. Caractacus reached the far door and pushed it open.

'The collection,' he said. 'Or part of it, at least.'

The room was the biggest Lexi and Al had ever seen. It was a huge hall, with its ceiling held up by rows and rows of stone columns, each with the face of a god carved into it. The columns went off into the distance, their tops lost in the smoke that was already growing thick near the ceiling. It was just possible to make out some kind of pattern up there, but not to see the detail.

'This way,' Caractacus said. 'Science.'

He checked the rows of shelves as they ran, reading the symbols on metal signs detailing the contents. He ducked down a row and counted his way along the scrolls. He pulled out three and then, two steps further along, three more. He handed them to Lexi.

'These are critical,' he said, then crouched down and pulled out two more. 'We must take these or there may be no dictionary and I'll just be a man with a couple of pigs

who's amazed each morning when the sun comes up. And perhaps you will be too, even in 2,000 years, if we lose it all.' He turned to Al. 'Next three rows, you and I grab whatever we can carry.'

The smoke was lower now, almost down to the top of the shelves. They could hear the fire in the next room, roaring as everything in there burnt. Caractacus told Lexi to wait at the end of the row while he and Al went to work.

He pushed a box into Al's hands.

'Archimedes,' he said, as he piled scrolls on top. 'And devices from Rhodes that show the position of stars and planets on any given date. The Egyptians are about to invent the mechanical clock but, if all this is lost, it won't happen for 1,400 years.'

'Really? A clock? In ancient Egypt?' The scrolls were almost up to Al's face.

'Who do you think came up with the idea of 24 hours in a day? The Egyptians.' He picked up more scrolls and undid the neck of Al's sack. 'What you're holding puts them only a few years away from a device to measure it. A clock.'

He pulled the bag open and Doug screeched and ran for safety as he shoved the scrolls in.

Caractacus turned back to the shelves, pulled down more scrolls and piled them into a fold in his robes.

'I think a rat might have got into your bag,' he said. 'Probably at my house. Sorry. Dark Ages. What can you do?'

There was a crash and the room filled with orange light, smoky shadows and a sudden wind that pulled at the shelves.

'A door's fallen in!' Lexi shouted as the fire hit the first shelves and the scrolls on them went up with a *whoosh*.

Caractacus turned and the scrolls in his arms bumped some boxes. One fell onto the floor and smashed. Fine metal instruments spilt across the tiles.

'Go!' he shouted. 'Go!'

He and Al ran to Lexi and the three of them skirted the wall all the way back to the dining-room door. Behind them, flames were rolling over the shelves and ash was being tossed through the air.

Caractacus led the way across the dining room to a statue of a man holding a scroll.

'Demetrius,' he said, as he pushed one hand down among the documents he was holding and took the silver peg from his pocket. 'First librarian here.'

With the peg, he tapped the tip of the rolled stone scroll in Demetrius's hand and a portal opened up. Silver light shone into the hazy air of the room. He drove the peg in, locked the levers and went to turn the key.

It broke off in the lock.

He stepped back, holding the useless end of the key up, not knowing what to do next.

'Well, that's never happened before,' he said. It was the very last thing Lexi and Al wanted to hear.

There was a cough behind and below Al's ear, a little ratty cough. Doug scrambled up onto his shoulder with a peg key between his teeth.

'It's from Harrow or Winchester,' Al said to Caractacus. 'Will it work?'

'Yes!' Caractacus said. 'Yes! It's the one bit that's the

same.' He took it and went to put it in the lock. He stopped. 'But the other key broke off in there. It won't go in.'

He reached for the broken piece of key, but couldn't pull it out. Lexi tried with her smaller hands, but her fingers kept slipping off. There was more smoke in the room now, and the fire burning through the collection was getting brighter, closer. Doug ran down Al's arm and onto his hand. Al held him up to the broken key and he took it in his teeth, but couldn't pull it out.

'I've got it.' Al said. 'Back in there. Those tools. They're our only chance.'

'But you—' Caractacus couldn't send him back in there. It was too dangerous.

'I'll be quicker than you would be.'

Caractacus knew there was no other way. 'Follow my voice,' he said. 'I'll go back in with you and wait by the door. If the smoke gets too thick, follow my voice to get out.'

He told Lexi to stay where she was, and he and Al set their loads down on the nearest table and went back to the door.

'Stay low,' Caractacus said. 'Stay below the smoke.'

'I know,' Al said. 'Science.'

He sounded braver than he felt. His heart was pounding even before he started running.

'There are 22 rows,' Caractacus shouted behind him. 'Count them as you go.'

Al ran and counted. If he bent down, his head was below the smoke and he wasn't too crouched to run. At row 22, he turned and saw scrolls on the floor, along with the models and instruments and the broken box they had been in. He went down on his knees, made a fold in his robes and packed them in the way Caractacus had. He took all the instruments he could manage, then stood up. His heel crunched down onto a model of the solar system.

He overbalanced, but steadied himself and ran from the shelves. A burning piece of manuscript fell on his shoulder, but he shook it off. The smoke was lower now and fires were breaking out everywhere. Something fell in his hair and he felt it singe. He shook his head and kept struggling forward.

'This way!' he could hear Caractacus's voice shouting. 'This way!'

The smoke was in Al's eyes and he could feel tears running down his cheeks. It was getting harder to breathe. He didn't know whether he would make it.

'This way!' The voice was closer now.

Al felt a hand take his arm. Caractacus pulled him into the dining room.

'Who's that?' Caractacus said, as he was about to shut the door.

Al turned and looked back at the shelves. He could just make out the shape of a man, moving between the rows with his arms full of scrolls.

'I know him,' Caractacus said. 'I think I know him.'

'Get us out of here!' Lexi shouted.

Al's eyes were still streaming as Caractacus helped him across the room. As they stood in front of Demetrius, he

could feel Caractacus rummaging through the instruments he had taken, but he could barely see him.

'Yes!' he heard him say.

Caractacus went to work, pulling and levering with the fine tools. The broken piece of key clicked, edged out a little and with one more move it fell onto the floor. Lexi stuck the new key in and turned it.

Al reached back to the table and picked up what he could. The portal glowed silver and then a dazzling white and, as he fell into it, everything in his arms slipped from his grasp. One object – something made of metal – seemed to make it into the portal but, when he tried to grab it, it too slipped away from him.

460

Northwic
East
Angle Lands

MAGNOVIEW

'I CAN'T BELIEVE you dropped it all,' Caractacus said as they sat on the ground next to the pigs.

Al was coughing and he still couldn't see properly. He felt sick.

'And I can't believe that you could make a stupid key that doesn't work, put our lives in total danger and then dare to criticise my brother when he saved us all! His rat was more useful than you in a crisis!' Lexi shouted. A minute ago, or a bit over 500 years, they could all have died. Almost dying was something she really, really wanted to stop doing.

Caractacus looked startled, but thought about what she'd said.

'Yes. You have a point.' He put his hand on Al's shoulder. 'What I meant to say was "well done". We'd all be Egyptians now if you hadn't managed that. Assuming we'd got out, of course.'

He took them into his house, poured three cups of the apple drink and a bowl for Doug, and bathed Al's eyes with liquid from a pale green bottle which was almost all neck. Al's vision cleared and he started to feel better.

'I've always thought it was the papyrus that was the problem,' Caractacus said. 'It grows right near Alexandria, so it was an obvious choice when they needed something like

paper. It certainly knows how to burn, though.' He took a mouthful of his drink. 'Still, paper does too. I suppose that room would have gone up quickly either way.' He was about to drink again, but stopped. He turned to Al. 'You did see that man, didn't you? Just before we left?'

'I think so.' Al tried to work out exactly what he had seen. 'Yes, there was a man. Running around getting scrolls, like us.'

'He looked to me like one of you. A word hunter. One I haven't seen for a long time.' He put his cup down on the table. 'But that can't be. Word hunters can only get to Alexandria on that night if they're with me. It must just have been someone who looked like him.'

He checked Lexi's scrolls and put them back on the shelf.

'You've done well too,' he said. 'You pair were a good choice.'

She didn't reply right away. He didn't much sound as if he meant it, and she thought he was being far too casual about what they had just been through. She could still smell smoke, and Al's burnt hair.

'How do you choose word hunters?' she said. She had spent most of the past two weeks wishing they hadn't been chosen, and she wondered if she could change his mind. 'What made you pick the two of us?'

'Oh, I didn't. The book chooses you,' Caractacus said, as if nothing could be done about it. 'You were Hunters already, though.'

'That's just a name.'

'I think you already know it isn't. A name isn't just a name.' He reached across the table and patted Doug. Doug kept drinking. 'You're all Hunters. The book needs people who can track and find something.'

'The "H"s,' Al said. 'The initials we keep seeing.'

'Yes, some hunters do that. It's a sign for others who might need it. Others leave things, small objects from the future. Things that won't stand out unless you're from the future yourself. It can help get a lost word hunter back on track, or give them somewhere to wait.' He topped up their drinks. 'Hunting's not without its risks. You know that already. You've seen a few battles. And some word hunters do get lost during their missions. Some hunters make badges of their peg keys so that lost hunters can recognise them and be put back on track. Not everyone gets through Hastings, but that's only part of it. Some just – seem to disappear. One or two get stuck. They don't find the transition point to the next time.'

'But why do people keep doing it, if it's so risky?' Al didn't like the way Caractacus talked about missing hunters as if he'd misplaced his number two measuring spoon. 'These are human lives you're talking about.'

'You already know the answer to that. And I regret every one of them, every hunter who goes astray. But each one keeps doing it because it's so important. Does English have a word to describe something that's hot in a spicy way? No, but it did and someone failed to hunt it. When you say "we" to someone, do they automatically know if they're included or not? No. There used to be two separate words – an inclusive "we" and an exclusive "we" – but someone failed to hunt the exclusive "we" and it was erased. It unexisted, in that moment. There is no record of it. It's not the same as less critical words fading away. *Cwylla, eorðgræf, hringwyll, pytt, séaþ* – all words for a well, as in a hole in the ground with water in it, but it's no disaster if your time only knows "well". But without the work of hunters, vital words would be lost in their thousands. There would have been a language crash long before your time, and a crash of society with it. You wouldn't have your phone. You wouldn't have any phone.' He waited a moment for it to sink in. 'Anyway, you two have done a good job of it so far. You could learn some sword-fighting skills, but you're already good at finding the transition points. I think you'll do very well.'

Al wondered if Caractacus said that to everyone.

'We've been calling those "portals",' Lexi said. She didn't want to talk about how important it was to keep hunting. 'The transition points. If you mean the "& more" things.' She was about to say that they'd got the idea from *Doctor Who*, but she'd already explained enough for one day.

'Portals.' Caractacus thought about it. 'I like that. It sounds – classical. It is classical, from the Latin, *porta*, gate. In two steps, I think. "Transition points" came from someone in the 20th century. Also Latin roots, I admit, but it's a bit short on poetry, isn't it? "Portals" is much nicer.'

'There was a voice,' Lexi said. Caractacus's talk of people getting stuck had reminded her. 'At the portal in Nantucket, in 1835. The word was "Hello". When Al put the peg in, a man on the other whaling ship – there were two ships – shouted out, "No," and I saw something golden.'

'Oh dear.' Caractacus sat back on his stool. 'If that something golden was a peg and he saw the portal, it sounds like another hunter on the same mission. It's not supposed to happen, but sometimes it does. Occasionally time doesn't mesh quite right, if you know what I mean.'

They had no idea what he meant.

'So, what's happened to him?' Al said, hoping the man was all right.

Caractacus thought about how to put it. 'He's probably still in Nantucket. The portal would have closed. It's not a lost cause, though. Another word hunter might find him, though I don't know how many words go through Nantucket at close to the right time – It's not a complete lost cause.' It was clear that he didn't think many words owed their existence to Nantucket.

'So we made it through, and because of that some poor guy's stuck in 1835?' Lexi said.

'You did what you had to do. And there are worse times to be stuck in than 1835. But now you know, you can keep a lookout. Wear a key as a badge. Who knows who you might find?' His finger hovered over the left side of his chest, showing where a key might go. 'Now, let's see what we've got. Let's see what we managed not to drop on our way out.' He opened one of the scrolls he had carried back, and started to read it. 'Oh, geometry. That'll be useful. I'll copy that.'

He spread his fingers across the scroll and started marking something out, swivelling his hand so that his thumb landed in different places.

'Can we go now?' Lexi said, not even trying to sound friendly.

'Oh, yes,' Caractacus said, as if he'd forgotten they were there. 'Any questions you want to ask before you do? I find this is a good time for questions.'

'Actually, we'd rather just go home.' Lexi had had enough. More than that, she knew that Al had had enough.

Al just nodded. He was tired and he wanted to be back

in his own century and to have a shower and stop smelling like smoke and a pig sty.

He emptied the scrolls from his sack onto the table, checked Doug was all right and took out the one remaining golden peg. They had left Winchester thinking they were only one step from home.

'I should get a bag,' Caractacus said to him. 'Maybe even a bigger one than yours. I could bring a lot more back that way.'

'Couldn't you have worked that out, like, a thousand years before now?' Lexi was still annoyed with him. He was some kind of time-travelling genius, but he hadn't worked out that he could carry more if he took a bag.

'Another good point,' Caractacus said. 'Look who's full of them. I am so going to enjoy working with you.'

He laughed, stood up and walked over to the door. He brushed the latch with his hand and it started to glow.

'Nothing more like a portal than a door,' he said. He waved for them to come over. 'I'm sure I'll be seeing you soon. Good luck until then. Keep the language alive.'

He stood back from the door as Al pushed the peg in and locked the levers.

'Better hope this key doesn't break!' Lexi said, turning to give Caractacus one last look.

And then they were gone.

They lifted and flew, in clear air and silver light. Every breath had a sharpness to it, and a surprising freshness. The pictures of future history rushed by until, far below, they saw an ocean's edge, a city, a creek lined by trees, and Fig Tree Pocket.

'Okay, do this,' Lexi said, swinging her arms around and banking, the way Caractacus had shown them.

Al followed her, and they swooped over the school and the freeway and the creek, down across their backyard and up over the railing onto the deck. Lexi checked the clock on her laptop.

'As usual,' she said, 'we've only just left.'

Al sat down. He felt Doug scramble out of his backpack and onto his shoulder. Doug looked around and sniffed at the smells of home – creek mud, gum trees, muffins. Someone nearby was baking muffins. He crawled under Al's collar and immediately fell asleep.

'You really gave it to Caractacus,' Al said to Lexi. He laughed at the thought of it, and the scowl she had kept on her face for that whole short stay in Northwic.

'He deserved it.' She wasn't backing off now. 'You saved us in that fire. His stupid key nearly had us stuck.'

'We could have got out the way we came in.'

'Out of the building, but not out of Alexandria. We'd be ancient Egyptians now. Or then.' It wasn't easy to talk about a future more than 2,000 years in the past. 'There would be no dictionary, who knows what language people would be speaking and what kind of shape it'd be in, and we wouldn't have a clue about it anyway because we'd be running round the streets of an ancient burning city with an annoying old man who couldn't even work out that he should have *brought a bag*.'

'I liked him.' Al wasn't sure 'like' was the right word, but it felt as if someone should stand up for Caractacus. 'He's kind of a wacky inventor. They don't always think in straight lines. And look at what he's doing. He wants to save language and knowledge. He's in a time when everything's gone wrong and he's totally focused on making a better future that he'll never live to see.'

'So, you want to do it?' Lexi knew they would have to have this conversation, but she didn't know it would happen right away. 'Next time that book goes off, you want to nosedive into the past with keys and pegs that may or may not work, fight in battles and all that? I mean, really, do we have to get stuck in every burning library that's ever been?'

'And what happens if we don't? What happens if we ignore it?'

The dictionary was next to Lexi's laptop, but neither of them wanted to look at it in case it started to glow again.

Lexi folded her arms on the table in front of her and put her head down on them. 'I don't know. That's what kills me. Another of those collapses he talked about? We end up living in a toilet – with pigs?'

Al turned her laptop around to face him. As he typed 'Library of Alexandria' into Google, the word 'burning' came up too. He clicked on the first couple of sites.

'The library stuff pretty much checks out,' he said.

'Of course it checks out. We were there.' She didn't lift her head. 'I think actually being there might even count for more than Wikipedia.'

'From the look of the pictures, everyone's guessing what the library looked like. I don't think anyone knows. They've got four possible times for the destruction by the fire. Ours was the first. Maybe they got it going again and someone else trashed it too.'

He clicked from one link to another to see what else he could find. There were pictures of Demetrius and lists of scholars and other librarians who had worked there. Then he found something he hadn't been expecting.

'Lex, look at this.' He turned the laptop round again.

On the screen was a device – a corroded clump of wheels and cogs.

'That's the thing you dropped in the portal,' she said. 'Or part of it, anyway, rusted up.'

It had been found in 1900 on a shipwreck off the Greek island of Antikythera. It had fallen out of the portal, but somehow fallen free of the fire, and ended up soon after that on a ship that might have been on its way to Rome, with treasures looted by Caesar.

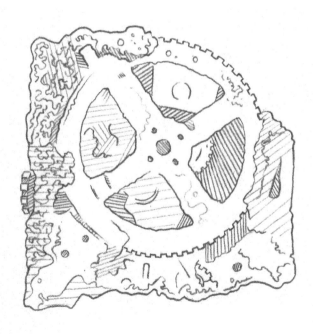

It took almost 2,000 years to be found and then another 50 years passed before someone worked out what it was – a computer to calculate the positions of the sun, moon and planets on any given day. It was made of hundreds of minute parts, with dozens of gears meshing with each other and dials with complex markings. It worked out the dates of eclipses, the years of Olympic games and the rising and setting of planets.

It was as sophisticated as a 19th-century Swiss clock, but such an idea made so little sense that it had been set aside and ignored until 1951. It predated European mechanical clocks by 1,400 years. In the early 20th century, it had seemed impossible that it could have existed at all 2,000 years before.

'That was just one bit,' Al said. 'One thing. That wasn't even the best bit.'

'Caractacus was right.' Lexi scrolled down the page and read more. 'They could have had clocks – regular 20th century clocks – in Egypt and Rome and Greece by about 40BC.'

'And computers by – when?' It was hard for Al to imagine how different the world might be.

'They could have had the internet before the Dark Ages. There wouldn't have *been* any Dark Ages.'

'So that's what happens when knowledge is lost. And all because the wind blew the wrong way one night in 48BC. That's Caractacus's point.' The artefact now known as the Antikythera mechanism made it obvious.

'So, we have to go on.' Lexi didn't want to admit it, but the risks of not going on suddenly looked too great.

They were word hunters now, and they had to accept it.

Later that evening, Lexi knocked on the door of Al's room when he was almost asleep. She was holding a framed photo.

'Here's why we have to go on,' she said. 'Forget everything else.'

He turned his bedside light on. It was a photo that was usually in the study. A family portrait from 30 years ago – the last one taken before their grandfather disappeared. Lexi was pointing to him.

There was a badge on the lapel of his suit. It was small, but there was no doubt about the shape. It was a peg key.

Their grandfather was a word hunter, and he was lost in the past.

CHRONICLE
OF THE
ENGLISH
LANGUAGES

Including some notable works
from each century

(by)

Caractacus of Northwīc
Advisor to several kings

525
Ecgbald writes Hengist
and Horsa first epic poem
in the new language
(Anglian dialect)
(not known to WHs
after 650)

Mid 5th century

~~nausea~~ ✝
'The Dark Ages'

430

Before 430
Thin air Brythonic
languages lost away
from time line
Old English yet to
evolve from
Angle, Saxon and
Proto-Germanic.

A timeline chart with entries above and below a central horizontal line marked with dates 600 and 1000.

Above the line (left to right):

Late 7th century
A feeling described by later WHs as like 'banking sideways' as Christianity comes to England and priests arrive in large numbers speaking Latin.

662–684
...odman writes poems, hymns and The Life of Saint Hilda in Northumbrian English (WHs report nine lines from one hymn survive in Bede's History of the English church (written in Latin and completed in 731). 21 ...ies still in existence in 1980 ...dest English work to survive, ...rvives in two dialects: West ...xon and Northumbrian in ...dition to Bede's Latin translation)

Up to late 10th century
small shudders felt by WHs on and off for two hundred years due to Viking raiders and settlers (words such as die, leg, sky)

890–900
Unusually smooth. ? likely due to King Alfred requiring more writing in English and more translation into English (learned work still in Latin)

960
Leif Halfdane writes The Saga of Eric Bloodaxe, King of Jorvik. Norse-style saga written in Northumbrian dialect (not known to WHs after 1020)

1224
Osbert writes Life of Aethelstan in Northumbrian dialect, but WHs report no copies known to exist after 1200

1066
The arrival of Normans and Norman French (described by WHs as a big shudder). Significant fall in new literature in English for 300 years

Below the line (left to right):

641
...enred writes Lives ...Kentish Kings ...report no longer ...n after early 8th ...s thought it may ...been the model for ...works documenting ...royal lines)

876
Haldric Half-Beard begins the Anglo-Saxon Chronicle (Haldric forgotten by 1000, but King Alfred orders copies made for all monasteries – copies independently updated from then, WHs confirm nine still in existence more than 1000 years later)

726
Leofwine and Aelfric write Beowulf, recording a story told since the events of 492 (WHs report authors no longer known soon after, and origins debated. The poem is later known from one surviving copy made in 1006. Edges burnt in fire in 1731, manuscript restored in 19th and 20th centuries)

1006
Odric Longtooth writes The Battle of Maldon (some of the poem is lost, but one incomplete manuscript of 325 lines survives until destruction in a fire in 1731, having been copied in 1724)

945
Eadwig writes the Battle of Brunanburh for King Edmund (WHs report poem recorded in four of nine remaining copies of the Anglo-Saxon Chronicle more than 1000 years later)

1287
Robert Lincoln writes Havelok the Dane, developed from earlier works (WHs report one imperfect version survives, and copies are made)

1382-1400
Geoffrey Chaucer writes, but does not finish, the Canterbury Tales

1400-1450
The Great Vowel Shift (felt by WHs as a swerve). Grandchildren and their grandparents sounded almost as if they were speaking different languages. Plural of foot shifts from fote to feet, a dwelling changes from hoose to house.
Cause of many English spelling peculiarities (spelling standardised in following centuries)

Mid-16th century
'Renaissance turbulence' new words arrive due to increased trade and travel (yacht from Dutch, yoghurt from Turkish), also inkhorn terms - big words from Latin and Greek that the language DIDNT NEED

Around 1600
The 'Shakespeare bump'. Shakespeare invents 1700 words (note - half still in use 400 years later, e[?] well-read, outgrow, unhelpful). Several other writers of the era invented hundreds of words each

1719
Daniel Defoe publishes The Life and Strange Adventures of Robinson Crusoe of York, Mariner called by some the beginning of the English popular novel. The first such work not derived from myths or histori[es]

〔 1400 〕 〔 1600 〕

1473
William Caxton prints Recuyell of the Histories of Troye the first book printed in English, though not in England. Set up printing press in England in 1476 and printed Chaucer's Canterbury Tales (see 1382-1400)

1476
Printing introduced to England by William Caxton. Books cheaper after this, more reading (CAN CHANGE A COUNTRY)
Before mid-1470s WHS reports a more rapid drop. Also, English starts to standardise to London East Midland English (with some variations) with increasing adoption of the Chancery Standard by printers

1524
Tyndale Bible first English Bible to be widely printed, introducing English into churches across the country, and promoting reading in English.

1623
Publication of Mr William Shakespeare's Comedies Tragedies and Histories (later better known as the First Folio. Written 1592-1616, WHs r[eports] 289 original copies still in existence 400 years later (millions of copies of individual plays in print from 19th century) Three other plays by Shakespeare also remain in existence 400 years later. [?] plays by Shakespeare include History of Cardenio, Loves La[bours] Won, King Alfred Parts I and Charlemagne (none k[nown to] WHs after 1800)

A timeline running horizontally with markers at 1800, 2000, and 2020.

Above the timeline:

1836
Charles Dickens publishes The Pickwick Papers, the first of 20 novels and numerous other works that see him called by some the greatest English novelist (comment made by 20th century WHs)

1755
Dr Samuel Johnson's A Dictionary of the English Language published with 200,000 quotations (not the first dictionary, but the first with such support) described by later WHs as feeling like a backfire/gearchange (? due to quotations)

1850 - 2010
Language manuals and prescriptive grammars 'feels like an obstacle course' all about RULES and not about BEING UNDERSTOOD. Language not about where the commas go (Note: it took 1000 years for English to find its first comma, so why be precious about them just because printers started throwing them about to impress? All just one person's preference becoming other people's rules. And words you can't end sentences with? Don't get me beginning.)

1920s
James Joyce's Ulysses, F. Scott Fitzgerald's The Great Gatsby and William Faulkner's The Sound and The Fury all published and subsequently regarded as among the ten greatest books of the century

1997
First publication of a paperless book using electronic coding (ebook)

Below the timeline:

1806
Noah Webster's Compendious Dictionary records American English

1817
Jane Austen's Pride and Prejudice is published, receiving three positive reviews. WHs report that Jane Austen becomes famous in the 20th century, and the book then sells 20 million copies, becoming one of the most loved books in English

1857
Unregistered Words Committee formed. Their work leads to the publication of the Oxford English Dictionary (12 volumes) in 1928, the most complete dictionary in history. Within 20 years, revision is underway LANGUAGE EVOLVES. The dictionary grows to have 600,000 entries.

2015-2020
Great Syntax Shift (following the globalisation of English and widespread use of hand-held signalling devices allowing message composition)

Late 1990s the emergence of TXT, a temporary abbreviated form of written English for hand-held signalling devices

WORD HUNTERS

THE LOST HUNTERS

NICK EARLS &
TERRY WHIDBORNE

$\mathcal{T}$HE LAST PHOTO of Alan Hunter was taken on the day he went missing. He taught year five at Cubberla Creek State School, and it was sports day. In the photo he wore an orange towelling hat, shorts which were pulled up way too high and socks that went to just below his knees. He had a megaphone in his hand and a vinyl bag over one shoulder with 'TAA' and a picture of a plane on it.

Even in that photo, Lexi thought she could see a word hunter's peg key pinned to her grandfather's shirt.

It was Lexi's turn to dust the lounge room, a job that always took ages because of the number of framed photos on the bookshelves. Al was on the back deck cleaning the barbecue. He complained every time that it was the worse job of the two, but he never wanted to swap.

Lexi took the photo of her grandfather into the kitchen, where their father was tying a bin bag.

'Do you know what that is?' She pointed to the key in the photo. 'I've always wondered.'

Al's face appeared at the window, glaring at her. He couldn't believe she'd brought it up, drawn attention to it.

Their father took the photo, then stretched his arm out and squinted at it. 'No. I'll need some help.' His reading glasses were at the end of the bench, and he put them on.

'Oh, that. It's a badge Grandad Al wore. He had it for a couple of years. He wore it a lot. I always assumed it was a Lions Club badge, or Rotary, or something.'

'I didn't know he was in any of those,' Al said through the screen. He had his hands next to his face to shut out the glare from outside.

'Well, I don't know that he was either.' Their father took another look at the photo. 'I don't remember him going to any meetings. I just thought that's what it was. I never asked him about it.' He handed the photo back to Lexi and waved his hand in front of his face at the smell of the rubbish in the bin bag. 'I've got to get this out of the house.'

He finished tying it and picked up the plastic recycling bin, which was full of bottles and crushed cereal boxes.

Al stayed at the window. As soon as their father was gone he said, 'What were you thinking? You could blow the whole thing.'

'Well, I didn't. And I wouldn't. Not with that.' Lexi put the photo down on the bench. 'We've got to find out what we can. Grandad Al is lost somewhere in the – I don't know – last few thousand years? Thirty years ago he chased a word into the past and it went wrong. The only people who know that, and the only people who have any chance of finding him, are you and me. And if I can find one clue in the present that'll get us to him sooner and save me from having to fight the Battle of Hastings again – or any other stupid war – I'll take it.'

The front screen door squeaked and slapped shut. Their father was back from the bins.

'Okay,' Al whispered before he came in. 'But there's got to be a better way to find him.'

About the Author

Nick Earls is the author of 15 books, including five novels with teenage central characters. *48 Shades of Brown* was a CBCA Book of the Year, and his other four young adult novels were Notable Books. *After January* was also shortlisted for the National Children's Literature Award, won a 3M Talking Book of the Year Award and was shortlisted in the Fairlight Talking Book Awards. The International Youth Library, Munich, included it in its White Ravens selection of international notable new books. It was the first of five of Nick Earls's novels to become plays. Two have also been adapted into feature films.

While the English origin of the name Earls is the old Saxon word 'eorl' or 'jarl', meaning 'village elder', in Nick's family's case it began somewhere totally different – in Arles in France. It's a place-based name. The family story behind it goes like this. When Hannibal of Carthage set out to attack Rome in 218BC, he established a base on the Rhone River before crossing the Alps. That base became a permanent settlement and took the Roman name Arelate, meaning 'town by the marshes'. Over time that name became Arles. (History records that some Greeks or Phoenicians were there before Hannibal, but the town was called Theline then.) Around 800 years ago, someone from Arles who had taken the place name as a family name moved to England. Over the years, various spellings emerged, 'Earls' among them.

About the Illustrator

TERRY WHIDBORNE has worked in the advertising industry for many years, and is now recognised as one of Brisbane's most award-winning senior Art Directors. But as Terry's family grew, so did his interest in illustration. He began developing his style for clients such as *Vogue*, Virgin Blue and many of London's top ad agencies, before deciding that what he really wanted to do was concentrate on books, film and animation. Terry's first foray into books is the Word Hunters trilogy he co-created with Nick Earls. He lives in Brisbane with his wife and two kids.

To be honest, Terry hasn't a clue where his family name comes from. Not that he hasn't tried to find out. But Nick, not for the first time, has a theory. Whidborne looks like a classic place name, but where is it? Nowhere. So Nick started factoring in spelling variations and thought 'Whid' and 'borne' had the look of old Anglo-Saxon (or possibly Celtic) words, though they weren't quite right. 'Hwit' – now written as 'Whit' – was though, and meant 'white'. After trying 'borne', 'born' and 'burn', he settled on 'bourne'. 'Whitbourne' meant 'white stream' and it turns out to be a town in Herefordshire in England.

ACKNOWLEDGEMENTS

In some kind of chronological order, I'd like to thank Ben Hayes for acting as my book consultant; Terry for jumping on board and for the ideas and talent he brought with him; Pippa Masson for all that clever behind-the-scenes agenting and the UQP team for connecting with what we were on about and taking it up a couple of gears – particularly Kristina Schulz and Mark Macleod for being exactly the editors I needed. I'm also grateful to Sarah and Patrick for their tolerance throughout as this became a much bigger and, I think, better thing.

NICK EARLS

What started off as a phone call from Nick has turned into a book trilogy of the most amazing stories. Thanks Nick for bringing me into your world of storytelling. A big thank you goes out to UQP, especially Kristina, for embracing the idea and also letting an unknown illustrator be part of such a big project. To Sue, Alec and Amy, for the support whilst I was hidden in the bunker. And lastly to Mitchell, my dog who kept me company throughout the day without chewing up any illustrations.

TERRY WHIDBORNE